The Chausie Cat

Chausie Cats Owner's Manual

Chausie's care, personality, grooming, health and feeding all included

by

Harvey Hendisson

Table of Contents

Table of Contents 3

Chapter 1: Introduction 4

Chapter 2: History of the Chausie 5

Chapter 3: General information about the Chausie 7

Chapter 4: Before you buy your Chausie............................14

Chapter 5: Choosing your Chausie 19

Chapter 6: Your new Chausie kitten or cat........................23

Chapter 7: Feeding your Chausie 40

Chapter 8: Grooming your Chausie 48

Chapter 9: Your Chausie's health 50

Chapter 10: Behavioural issues 98

Chapter 11: Becoming an Chausie breeder 112

Chapter 12: The aging Chausie cat 123

Chapter 13: Prices and costs 127

Chapter 14: General advice & tips 131

Conclusion 134

Chapter 1: Introduction

The Chausie is the result of a breeding program that crossed the Jungle Cat with the Abyssinian, the Bengal, and the Oriental Shorthair. It is its wild cat ancestor, the Jungle Cat or *felis chaus* that gave its name to the breed. While there were many Chausies produced as a result of Jungle Cats and domestic cats mating over the centuries, formal breeding only began as recently as the 1990's. We now have a wonderful new breed with a 'wild' look but a domesticated nature. The personality of the Chausie has been likened by some to that of the otter: active, agile, intelligent, playful and water-loving! They are also loving, affectionate, sociable, outgoing, fearless and demanding. These cats don't do well when left alone too often or for too long. The Chausie's appearance has been compared to that of wild cats, specifically the cougar and the lynx thanks to their lean and muscular bodies, long muzzles, high cheekbones, long legs and the tufts of hair on the ends of their ears.

Please note that some of the information in this book is not specific to the Chausie but can be applied to all breeds of cat. However, much of the details and tips are breed specific. I hope you find this book useful and fun to read!

Chapter 2: History of the Chausie

1) The history and origin of the Chausie cat

The Chausie, sometimes spelled "Chaussie" and pronounced *chow-see*, traces its origins back to the Jungle Cat of Northeast Africa and Southeast Asia. It is the Jungle Cat that also lent its Latin name, *felis chaus*, to the breed of domestic cat we know today.

Evidence of the Jungle Cat has been found in many artefacts from ancient Egypt including paintings, writings, and actual cats that had been mummified. These seem to indicate that these wild cats had been domesticated by the Egyptians who thought highly of them. Some believe that the statues of the Egyptian goddess Bastet were modelled on these elegant, long-legged felines. There are also clear indications that the Jungle Cat had mated with the ordinary domestic cat, *felis catus*, in many countries and over several centuries.

It was not until 1960 that the first formal breeding between a Jungle Cat and an ordinary domestic cat was carried out. It is not known how or why these cats came to the attention of breeders. It is also unclear who the first breeder or breeders were. However, what is known is that the early pioneering breeders crossed the Jungle Cat with the Abyssinian, the Bengal, and the Oriental Shorthair. Breeders only began working together in the 1990's.

In 1997 the breed had advanced and the only permissible outcross breeds became the Abyssinian and the humble domestic cat. These splendid cats are now being bred in North America and several European countries.

Once the Chausie had achieved Championship status, outcrosses with other breeds were no longer permissible for cats that are used as show cats.

2) *The status of the breed*

The International Cat Association (TICA) granted the Chausie foundation registry status in 1995. In 2001 this was changed to New Breed Class. On May 1, 2013 this gorgeous breed was awarded full Championship status.

When full championship level was achieved breeders could no longer outcross with other breeds if they wanted to show their cats. To be shown a cat must have three generations of pure Chausie behind them or be three generations away from their 'wild' Jungle Cat ancestors to qualify.

Breeders are also in the process of having these splendid cats accepted by the World Cat Federation (WCF). At this stage, however, TICA is the only association with which the Chausie is registered and recognized.

3) *The 'wild' cat misrepresentation of the breed*

There are some individuals who have experienced the Chausie as aggressive, hyperactive, unpredictable and destructive and claim that it is because the breed has wild cat DNA.

One can argue there are individual domesticated cats of all breeds that are like this due to poor or no socialisation when they were kittens or being badly treated at some point in their lives.

In order to give a more balanced view of this issue, though, one must acknowledge that there is a chance that a Chausie will exhibit some undesirable behaviours and / or not exhibit some desirable ones if he or she is only one or two generations away from the Jungle Cat breeding animal. For this reason it is important to get proof from a breeder that a kitten has enough pure Chausie in its past to put distance between it and the Jungle Cat.

Chapter 3: General information about the Chausie

1) The Chausie's personality

The Chausie's personality is at odds with its 'wild' cat appearance because they are extremely affectionate cats that form very strong bonds with their owners. They are very intelligent, loving, playful (this lasts well into adulthood), fun, good-natured and sociable. They are assertive cats and will make sure that their owner knows what they want. They get on well with cats and with cat-friendly dogs but they are not an ideal breed for families with very young children because of how boisterous they can be. What may put some people off is that they are extremely active cats although adults are not quite as 'busy' as kittens are. These cats demand their owner's attention and involvement. While their agility, athleticism and energy make them really entertaining to watch, they can also be a bit exhausting. It is advisable to set limits and establish a routine when a Chausie is still young.

2) The Chausie's appearance

The Chausie is a shorthaired, medium to large cat that is very athletic in build. Some owners describe them as looking like basketball players thanks to their long, strong legs that were designed for jumping and running. These cats also have long bodies.

Their long legs, large but slender and flat-sided bodies, deep chests, slanted cheekbones and long muzzle, and tufted ears make them look both elegant and powerful at the same time. These cats have both grace and power.

The breed standards for the Chausie set by TICA allow three colours: solid black, black ticked, and brown ticked:

> ➢ In the brown ticked tabby each hair is banded: light at the skin, black at the level of the base coat, alternating light bands up the hair shaft and ending with a black tip.

> ➢ Solid black Chausie kittens sometimes have tabby markings that are very faint but discernible none the less. However, by the time they are mature adults they have become a deep and even black. As with any black cat, a great deal of exposure to sunlight over the course of several years may fade the black until it is more a very deep chocolate brown.

> ➢ The grizzled, ticked black tabbies are often born black. As they get older the tabby markings begin to emerge. These lovely tabbies often have a background coat that is a dark, brownish-black. However, the background colour could be a light golden brown, beige, a reddish gold or even a light grey with only a hint of brown in it. Regardless of the background colour the tabby stripes are pure black.

3) Chausie Breeding Standards

The breeding standards for the Chausie that are used by judges at cat shows and breeders are:

> ➢ *Head and face*: The head is medium in width and wedge-like. The forehead is sloping and long and the cheekbones are high and angular. The muzzle, too, is long. The chin is full and the jaw is strong. The nose is medium to wide and the nose leather is rounded.

> *Ears*: The ears are large, tall and erect and set at a slight outward angle. The ears are wide and end in rounded tips, preferably with ear tufts of dark hair.

> *Eyes*: Medium to small in size. The top of the eye is flattened and the bottom is rounded making the eye look like a half oval. The ideal eye colour is gold or yellow but light green or hazel eyes are also accepted.

> *Neck*: Medium in terms of both length and thickness.

> *Body*: Large, lean, long and flat-sided with a deep chest and firm musculature.

> *Legs:* Long and medium-boned.

> *Paws*: Medium sized and oval.

> *Tail*: Medium in width and a little short. The taper is slight.

> *Coat*: The undercoat is soft and dense and the outer coat feels coarser the greater the degree of grizzling in the coat.

> *Colour and patterns:* Three variations: brown ticked tabby, solid black and black grizzled, ticked tabby. With all three the nose leather is black and paw pads are black, pink or a combination of black and pink.

4) Life span

A Chausie that is well cared for and fed correctly will live for between 14 and 20 years!

5) Intelligence

The Chausie is without question an intelligent cat. They are easy to train thanks to this, their natural curiosity and the fact that they really enjoy their owner's company and attention. They love games like fetch and can be easily trained to walk on a leash or lead, do tricks of various kinds, and run agility courses.

Their intelligence and high energy levels mean that they need stimulation and interaction to be healthy and happy.

6) *How often to play with your Chausie*

If you pose this question to your Chausie it will reply, "All the time that I'm not eating or sleeping!" These cats love playing and can be demanding. They need companionship, activity and stimulation. If it can't come from their owner it needs to be supplied by another pet and games such as puzzle games.

The Chausie that gets cuddles, lots of attention and playtime will be a very happy, loving and relaxed cat and a truly wonderful companion for many years.

7) *The amount of space they need*

Despite the fact that the Chausie is an energetic and agile cat it doesn't necessarily require a great deal of space. In fact, they are curious, bold and fearless and these qualities can get them into dangerous situations out of doors.

All the physical activity and mental stimulation that the athletic Chausie needs can be supplied through play.

8) *Indoor versus outdoor cats*

Contrary to popular belief it isn't cruel to keep a cat indoors. In addition, a breed like the Chausie where your cat is focused on you rather than the space it inhabits will be happy to be inside and with you. There are many reasons why keeping a cat indoors is preferable, especially fearless breeds like this one.

Outdoor cats, especially those that roam, are at much greater risk of picking up infections from the other cats. Not all cats your cat will come in contact with outside will be vaccinated or healthy. No cat owner wants to expose their cat to the danger of possibly contracting a fatal illness such as Feline Leukaemia or Feline

Immunodeficiency Virus, both of which are easily transmitted and fairly common in cats that roam outside.

In addition to the risk of infection is the danger of injuries as a result of fights with other cats including strays or even feral cats. Some bites can lead to abscesses, which can make a cat really sick very fast. Other illnesses such as rabies can be passed on by a bite or scratch from an infected cat.

Other cats are not the only animals that pose a potential threat to your Chausie. Domesticated cats that wander from their home are usually not able to defend themselves against animals like dogs, opossums, foxes and snakes. These encounters will often either result in serious injuries or even death immediately or some time later as a result of infection. If your cat wanders into the wrong areas it becomes vulnerable to attacks from any of these creatures that are either defending a territory or acting from fear or aggression. The other potentially dangerous creatures out there are people who have been known to poison, shoot or otherwise injure or kill cats.

Cats that roam around outside are also inevitably going to encounter further danger: roads and traffic. Although many cats are smart enough to avoid the sound of approaching vehicles, a cat might run across a road if frightened by something such as a dog or a loud noise. In most cases an encounter with a motor car will result in very serious injury or death on impact.

Threats to your cat also come in the form of parasites such as fleas and ticks and fungi such as ringworm. Undergrowth, sand and stray or untreated cats harbour ticks and fleas. Both of these insects could potentially get onto your Chausie. Fleas carry diseases that can make your cat and you unwell.

Ticks are even more dangerous as certain types can paralyze or even kill a cat if not treated correctly. Tick bites for humans can cause serious illness too. A cat that wanders around outdoors could also pick up ringworm, which is easily transmitted to

11

people. This is not a serious or life threatening problem but it is not easy to treat and tends to recur as a result.

A further danger facing an outdoor cat is getting lost. Cats can get distracted by an interesting scent, chase after a small animal or another cat and then lose its bearings. It is best not to dwell on the possibility that your Chausie could get stolen but it could happen. Even individuals who don't realise the value of a cat may take it because they like it, think it's a stray or to use for appalling things like to sell to a laboratory that does testing on animals. While the chances are small, why take the risk?

Keeping a cat indoors also avoids the potential for disputes with neighbours and ill-feeling. A cat might decide that a flower bed next door makes the ideal outdoor litter box. While performing the necessary excavations, plants might be uprooted or damaged. Even if there's no damage your neighbour is unlikely to be charmed with the new type of manure being deposited in her or his garden by your cat!

There's also the possibility that your cat could get into a fight with a neighbourhood cat and you might be expected to pay the resulting vet bills. Finally, your male cat might not be popular if he impregnates the cat next door.

Keep in mind that the most important thing in your cat's life will be you. This means that your Chausie cat, whether male or female, will be more than happy to be a home-body if you are there and if he or she has some company, or at least a few toys, and enough food and water when you are out. Given they are very intelligent and curious these cats are unlikely to get bored and playing with them will give them enough exercise and stimulation to keep them fit physically and emotionally.

Given all of these factors in favour of keeping your cat inside it is hardly surprising to learn that indoor cats have much healthier and longer lives that their outdoor counterparts. If you are reluctant, however, to keep your cat inside but don't want your Chausie to roam there is the option of building a cat enclosure.

A cat enclosure is much more than a cage. Regardless of the amount of space you have available outside, you can create a really fun and safe outdoor area for your Chausie. It will of course have to be enclosed and you need to use cat proof fences. The height of a fence is a consideration too as a cat can leap five times its own height from a standing position.

You could either build an enclosure yourself or purchase one. If you have a significant amount of space – and a fair bit of money – available, a cat enclosure can be large enough to include ramps, sleeping platforms, tunnels for play, tree branches and so on. Remember to provide both warm and shaded spots.

An alternative, if you have less space, is a cat run. This could be an enclosed narrow strip down the side of a house or an enclosed veranda or balcony. With a smaller space such as a balcony you could use cat netting. Again, the addition of objects such as branches, platforms or tunnels to climb up, onto or through will make it a fun, stimulating place for your cat.

Regardless of whether you have an enclosure or run for your Chausie, you must make sure that it has easy and safe access to it through a window or cat flap.

If the enclosure is some distance from the house, you could consider an enclosed tunnel from the point of exit from your home to the enclosure. This way your cat has exercise just getting to and from its outdoor enclosure!

9) The Chausie's average size and weight

The Chausie is a medium sized cat with a long, muscular body. The males typically reach 15 to 25 lbs (6.8 to 11 kg) and the smaller females weigh between 10 and 20 lbs (4.5 to 9 kg).

Chapter 4: Before you buy your Chausie

1) Questions to ask before bringing an Chausie home

The first issue you need to consider before buying a Chausie, or any other pet for that matter, is whether you are prepared and able to be a responsible owner. There are several lifestyle factors that a potential Chausie owner must consider:

1. **Time**: a Chausie kitten or cat needs and will in fact demand play time from you. These cats are not at all good at being left alone so if you are out each day you are urged to get another cat and provide lots of games and toys.

2. **Environment**: are there things in your environment which pose a danger to an animal? If there are any hazards in the environment, are you able to easily remove these?

3. **Cost**: the first significant cost is the price you will have to pay for the Chausie kitten or cat that you choose. Thereafter there will be regular expenses including food, vet or medical expenses, grooming products and other incidentals such as bedding, toys, scratching post et cetera.

4. **Patience**: litter box training is fairly quick with most breeds but with a kitten there are likely to be a few accidents at first. Also, as with any boisterous and playful animals a 'busy' Chausiekitten may knock over and break items. Adults are active too so there may be the odd mishap… You need to deal with these issues without becoming impatient or punishing your cat.

2) The shopping list for your new kitten or cat

There are several items that should, preferably, be acquired before you fetch your Chausie and bring your new companion home.

Food and related items

The first item is food. Obviously the type of food you purchase will depend on whether you are going to bring a kitten or a cat home; different aged cats have differing nutritional needs. It is recommended that you purchase a mixture of canned food and dry food. Like people, cats enjoy a varied diet. On the can or the bag of food it will clearly state the age of the cat that the food has been formulated for.

Some Chausie owners are great supporters of a diet of bones and raw food for their cats. However, this is not recommended with very young cats.

In addition to the food itself, you will need to purchase food and water bowls. It's always a good idea to have more than one per cat so that you can insure that you have a clean bowl to use at all times. As you are not going to be with your cat all the time, it can be a very good idea to purchase an automatic food dispenser. This way your cat will not be without food at any stage during the day or night.

Cat Litter

There is a vast array of cat litters available commercially. The general rule of thumb is to avoid scented litters; while you might prefer them it's highly unlikely that your cat with its highly developed sense of smell will. Cat litters that clump are also to be avoided, especially if you have a young cat that might eat some of the litter and subsequently suffer from blockages in the digestive system.

Working out what the best litter is for your cat is a question of trial and error. Eventually you will find the one that your cat responds to best and that you don't find too onerous to clean or replace. If you ever run out of clean cat litter an emergency measure that works very effectively is either soil or sand from your garden or shredded newspaper.

Bed and bedding

While it's not always necessary to buy bedding for a cat it can be a good idea. Of course, you might buy a bed that will then be ignored in favour of a couch, the floor, a chair or your bed! Most Chausie cats really enjoy sharing their person's bed unless the weather is very warm.

Toys

There is also a wide range of toys available for cats and kittens that vary in sophistication and cost. You could certainly choose one or two of these to have at your home for when your new charge arrives.

Alternatively, it is not always necessary to buy toys as one can make them. For example, a kitten or cat will have hours of enjoyment chasing the end of a piece of string, jumping up to catch a cork or a small ball suspended by piece of string. It is perhaps better to get to know your cat a little before deciding what sort of toys he or she is likely to respond to best.

Scratching post

It's not only important for your cat to have a scratching post to keep their claws sharp, you and your furniture need this piece of equipment too because your cat is far less likely to sharpen its claws on your furniture. A scratching post is necessary to help keep your cat's claws healthy too. And it's another item to play with…

Clothing

Opinion is divided about clothing for cats in general. Many cat owners believe that clothing is unnatural on a cat and it just causes the animal stress and, in the worst case scenario, an adverse skin reaction.

3) Removing household hazards

Medicine

One of the most toxic substances for a cat is your prescription medications or drugs. They are in fact the most common cause of poisoning in cats. For instance, an ingredient like ibuprofen, which is found in many painkillers, is deadly for cats.

Just as you would for children, you must ensure that all drugs or medications are kept where your cat cannot find them and ingest them.

Electrical appliances

While it's not always possible to remove electrical appliances or their cords, one needs to take care with them because kittens and young cats like playing with moving or dangling objects. An electrical cord attached to an iron, for example, will be irresistible to a young kitten. Your cat will pull on the cord or swing from it.

This could be very dangerous for both the cat and your property. In addition, if the cat's teeth penetrate the cord's plastic covering he or she will receive an electric shock.

Poisons

Cats are foragers by nature. Chausie cats are very curious and adventurous cats so it is very important that you don't leave any garden pest powders, pellets and sprays; weed killers; cleaning materials; contaminated foods or foods toxic to cats exposed and accessible. If you do, your cat will find them and, although they are not indiscriminate eaters, there is a chance that poison could be ingested.

Poisonous plants

There are certain plants you may have in a garden or indoors or potted plants that are poisonous or potentially deadly for cats. In fact, the list of plants toxic to cats is astonishingly lengthy. It includes Rhododendrons and Azaleas, Lily-of-the-Valley, the lily family, Amaryllis, Holly, Asparagus Fern, Begonia, Clivia, Chrysanthemums and Cycads to name just a few. A general rule of thumb is that plants with variegated leaves should be avoided, as they are more toxic than others.

It is possible that your Chausie will decide to snack on a pot plant, especially if it is an indoor cat. You will have to decide how great a risk the plants you have pose.

Swimming pools

If you have a swimming pool, a secure pool cover is a good idea while your cat is young. Don't ever leave a kitten near a pool or even a pond unattended. If your neighbour has a pool or pond there's not much you can do about it. However, once your cat is settled, you can and should teach it about pool safety (see the relevant section of "Training" in chapter 6).

Doors and windows

When you bring your new kitten or cat home for the first time you must see that all the windows and external doors are closed. Any cat that is confronted by new sights, sounds, smells and people may panic and dash about initially. The last thing you want is for a frightened cat to vanish through an open door and window!

Heat sources

Some sources of heat are dangerous for a cat to be around. You need to take precautions to prevent your cat being burnt. You need to be careful with stoves, stove hot plates, heaters, exposed light bulbs, fireplaces and the inside of large appliances that may be warm. Your cat may cosy up to any one of these and not realize till it's too late that its delicate skin has been affected.

Try to screen open or accessible heat sources within the home and close appliances such as tumble dryers so your cat can't climb in.

Chapter 5: Choosing your Chausie

Choosing the Chausie that is going to become your companion is both important and difficult. This is especially the case if you are confronted by a number of kittens, each with its own personality and characteristics. Selecting a kitten using the, "Ooh! That one is *so* cute!" method is not good enough. You must take your time to find the kitten that is right for you.

While much of your decision will be based on the kitten or cat itself, if you are getting a kitten from a breeder then he or she will also impact on your choice. If the breeder has socialized the kittens they will be happy – or at least comfortable – to be picked up and handled. If the kittens aren't and seem fearful of people or nervous this is an indication that they have not been well treated and may exhibit behavioural problems now and / or later in life.

You should also establish which generation the Chausie kitten or cat you are interested in is. A first generation cat is still very close to its feral roots and may be a real handful! A second generation cat will be significantly less 'wild' and will be a true domestic cat. Third generation Chausies are pure breeds and 100% domesticated. They are also potential show cats.

You also need to assess the kitten or cat's state of health. Have a careful look at the eyes, which should be clear and bright. Make sure that there is no discharge from its eyes, ears or nose. The gums and tongue should be pink. Watch that the kitten's gait is even. Ensure that the kitten has good hearing and eyesight by making a noise and moving your finger. If the kitten turns to the sound and follows the movement it means their sight and hearing are fine.

After you have looked at health and general behaviour you can sit back and watch the kittens play and interact, look at markings and eye colour if that is important to you, and consider things such as personality, energy levels and curiosity.

It is worth taking your time to choose the kitten that will be right for you. The wrong choice may result in having to return the kitten, which will be upsetting for you and traumatic for the kitten.

1) General considerations

Getting one or two cats

As stated previously, Chausie cats are sociable and loving. They need company and interaction and stimulation. Getting two cats is therefore a good idea if you will be out at work all day.

Buying a male or a female

This is a hotly debated question and it can be an important consideration. Some believe that male and female cats are cast in similar stereotypical moulds as their human counterparts: males are more physical, even aggressive, and females are gentler.

Many people want a female because they assume it will be more loving and sweeter. However, many believe that one should choose a kitten or cat based on health and personality; don't let gender be the deciding factor.

The age a kitten should be when you buy it

A reputable breeder won't allow anyone to take a kitten that is younger than 12 weeks old. Ideally a Chausie will only be released when it is between 12 and 16 weeks old.

This delay is because the kittens need to be weaned correctly, have time to get strong, to be socialised and to have the required vaccinations and deworming.

A registered versus a non-registered kitten

If you obtain a kitten from a registered and reputable breeder, a registered kitten comes with a number of advantages.

Firstly, you know that your Chausie kitten is actually a purebred Chausie. Secondly, you can rest assured that the kitten is old enough to leave its mother and it has been socialized. In addition, a registered cat is far less likely to carry genetic or other illnesses. A professional breeder will also have had the necessary vaccinations done and the kitten will be dewormed.

With an unregistered kitten you have none of these assurances; there's no guarantee the kitten is either healthy or even really a Chausie.

2) What to ask the breeder

When you talk to breeders, either when you are selecting one or before choosing your Chausie, there are a number of issues you need to discuss and investigate.

The breeder and the facility

To begin with, you want to know about the breeder and the facility. You need to ask to see proof of his or her registration as a Chausie breeder.

A tour of the breeder's premises is also recommended. Where are the cats housed? Are the rooms, runs or areas the cats are in clean, airy and spacious? If a breeder refuses to let you look around, leave!

The kitten or cat's lineage and the breeding pair

You should ask the breeder about the kitten's lineage, including the age of the mother and father because cats should not be bred past a certain age.

You also want assurances, and preferably proof, of the health of the breeding pair in terms of vaccinations and overall health. If you intend to show your cat you should also establish if the parents have ever been shown as this indicates breed standard.

Meeting the breeding pair will also help you to get an idea of the size their offspring will reach and also give you an indication of personality as the mother in particular influences this.

Medical documentation

Finally, request proof from the breeder that the kitten has had its vaccinations, been dewormed and declared fit by a vet. The breeder must also provide you with a health guarantee. If he or she refuses, be suspicious.

Lineage

As previously mentioned, it is important to establish the Stud Book Traditional (SBT) status of a kitten. You need to know if it is a first generation (F1), second, third or fourth generation Chausie.

The kitten's temperament

This, too, will be hinted at by the temperament and nature of the kitten's mother and the SBT status. However, the breeder will have – or should have – spent a lot of time with the kittens. Ask him or her about the temperament and personality of the kittens on offer or of the one that you are interested in.

Of course, your own observations while you watch the kittens play and when you interact will also tell you a lot about them. It is not hard to see which kittens are shy, extroverted, adventurous, and playful and so on. You know what you are looking for in your Chausie companion so watch for those qualities.

Chapter 6: Your new Chausie kitten or cat

1) The first important few hours

It is recommended that when you get home with your new Chausie you restrict him or her to just one or two rooms initially. Firstly, too much too soon can be overwhelming for a kitten or even an adult cat whose sense of hearing and smell is far more acute than ours. Secondly, housetraining is a little easier for you if your kitten is not allowed to go everywhere at the beginning. Finally, it allows you to bond with your cat and have control over how and when your Chausie meets the other members of the household.

Don't be concerned or offended if your new kitten or cat's first act when you get home is to go into hiding. It might choose to crawl back into the carrier it arrived in or find another spot. It's not a bad idea to provide a few hiding spots that are easy to get in and out of. When your new Chausie is ready it will emerge and begin to cautiously explore the new room it finds itself in. Don't force the issue; wait till he or she is ready to come out of hiding.

It can be a good idea to close the new arrival into this room and leave it on its own for an hour or so to give it a chance to calm down. Make sure that you have placed food and water in the room along with bedding and a cat litter box. Keep in mind that cats are clean creatures so don't place the cat box near the food and water bowls. Leaving a few toys in the room will also help your new companion begin to relax.

You must never reach for the cat or try to cuddle in the beginning. If your cat is not nervous by nature, it may just come to you on its own. What you should do, however, is visit the cat regularly. Walk into the bonding room, sit on the floor or a low seated chair for a while and call out to him in a voice that is soothing. It is okay for you to walk in and out of the room as long as you leave your kitten or cat alone for a couple of hours in between. Even if

23

it takes several sessions to get your cat to even greet you, don't lose your patience.

In case there are children in your family, make sure that they visit the cat only when they are accompanied by an adult. At least in the initial days, this is mandatory. The reason to take this precaution is that children might get excited at the sight of the cat. If they startle the cat, he might just become anxious and even scratch or harm the child. So, never let children near the cat without proper supervision.

2) Settling in

Bringing your new Chausie home for the fist time is both exciting and a little scary. It should be the start of a wonderful, long relationship so one must begin well. Keep in mind that there is a great deal that is new for the kitten or cat to adjust to; don't try and do it all at once.

If you work, try to collect your kitten or cat at a time, like a Saturday morning, that allows you to spend an extended period with him or her to make the transition easier and so you can bond. The time you take to bond with your new Chausie is an important investment in your relationship that will stand you both in good stead for many years to come. You need to take the time and make an effort to get to know each other.

As mentioned, cats have very acute hearing and smell. Your home is going to present your new Chausie with a host of sounds and smells that are new and sometimes intimidating. Things that are ordinary to us will sound very loud and scary to a newly arrived kitten or cat. To help him or her with this, there are a few guidelines to follow.

When you talk to your new kitten do so softly and don't pick it up too often. The sound and smell of you is new, too. Also, don't play music or the TV very loud. Wait to use the vacuum cleaner until your Chausie has bonded with you and started to settle in. At

24

the very least, don't vacuum the room your kitten or cat is placed in when it first arrives so that it has a non-threatening space to be in. Hosting parties or dinner parties and having a line of people trooping in and out to admire or meet your new cat is also not a good idea.

3) Bringing home an adult Chausie

An adult cat needs to be treated differently to a kitten. You need to take a few additional steps before bringing an adult Chausie home.

First, an adult cat will usually take a little longer to settle than a kitten. Why? Because adult cats, like adult people, have a history and past experiences that result in established patterns of behaviour along with likes and dislikes. If you can find out what these are it will help you and your new Chausie. If you get your cat from a breeder you can find about its past and interactions with people and other animals. If your new cat comes from a shelter you may not be able to get any information and will have to be guided by your cat's reactions.

You can also ask about food, toy and activity likes and dislikes. Being able to provide things you know your new companion is familiar with and enjoys will help him or her settle more easily. You could also enquire about things that the cat finds frightening. For instance, I once acquired a cat who was affectionate, laid-back, funny and usual fairly fearless. However, he was terrified of plastic grocery bags! At the sound or sight of one he would run. Somewhere in his past something unpleasant with a plastic bag had happened. I made a point never to have one anywhere near him.

Adult cats, if necessary, can be kept in a cat carrier for a few days. The carrier should be placed in the room that the cat will be confined to once it leaves the carrier. In fact, the carrier can be left in an out-of-the-way place permanently for use by your cat when it feels frightened, anxious or under the weather.

Just as with a kitten, there must always be food – preferably one the cat is familiar with and likes – and fresh water available. A litter box is also necessary. When kittens and cats are accustomed to the sound and scent of their new owner it's important to spend as much time as possible with it as part of the settling in phase.

Once there is less likelihood of accidents, and your new Chausie has left the room it was initially confined to, it's a very good idea to keep your kitten or cat company as it explores the entire home. Only when it has examined everything and every room will it decide which spots will be its resting, sleeping and hiding places.

Your new adult Chausie needs to be watched. If your cat is not eating or using the litter box, showing signs of restlessness or scratching or licking excessively you may need to consult a vet as these are possible signs of stress and unhappiness.

4) Preparing your family for a pet

It is not only you and your home that must be ready for your new arrival. Everyone in the house must be prepared. Young children especially are usually so delighted to see a pet that they might shout, rush at or attempt to pick it up. This would not be what your Chausie needs!

All the occupants of your home need to be informed about the cat that will be joining the household: when it will arrive, what it will look like, the changes that must be made both during the settling in phase and afterwards, to be patient and give the cat time and space to adjust and not to expect or try to handle or play with it immediately. With the Chausie the waiting period before it is ready to have social and fun time with the family shouldn't be too long as they are so playful, sociable and gregarious by nature.

You will also need to make sure everybody knows about feeding, the litter box requirements, not feeding the cat unhealthy treats, keeping medicines and other poisons safely put away and keeping doors and windows closed until the initial period is safely negotiated.

Also, given cats love to explore and will sometimes go to sleep in odd places, the family must get into the habit of checking inside big appliances such as washing machines, tumble dryers and dishwashers before turning them on.

5) Make time for your new cat

The Chausie cat loves affection but it's not necessary to play with it immediately. In fact, until it is feeling relaxed and settled it is unlikely to feel like playing, but you must spend time in the same room with it and speak to it in a friendly and soothing tone.

Just sit in the room and give your new companion time to get used to your scent and the way you sound, look and move. Family members can take turns spending time with the new arrival but at the beginning it should just be you.

Playtime

This can start in earnest with your new cat once it is used to the new surroundings. How can you tell? Your Chausie will emerge from hiding and want to include you in his or her territory. You will know you have been accepted and marked when your new companion rubs its head, body or face on you to leave their scent. You are now their person!

Even if your new cat now rubs itself against your legs it may still resist overtures from you. If you reach out to stroke or touch the cat or kitten and it backs off you can either leave it and give it a little more time or your could lure it with toys… A shoe lace or piece of string pulled along the ground is pretty irresistible to the majority of cats who will immediately chase and pounce. A high energy and interactive game like this is the ideal ice breaker between you and your new Chausie.

6) Complicated scenarios

You will have to do a little extra work if you are introducing your new Chausie into a household in which there is a child, a dog or

27

another cat or cats. This is because if there are other animals there are hierarchies and pecking orders already in place that your new arrival will have to fit into. However, there are steps one can take that will make the transition much smoother for all concerned.

Introducing your Chausie to your dog

Another of the many advantages of this breed is that they get on well with dogs. That is assuming of course that the dog is cat-friendly. No breed will be comfortable with a dog that thinks cats are for chasing or make great snacks! If you are not quite sure how your dog will behave there are a few things you can do to make sure that there are no problems.

While your new Chausie is in the bonding room for the post-arrival period don't let the dog in. What does help is to get them used to each other's scents or pheromones before they meet in person. An easy way to achieve this is by feeding them on either side of the door. Of course if your dog starts barking or scratching at the door you must move him or her further away and then move the bowl closer to the door again gradually. Eventually they will become familiar with each other's smell. It's time to move on to the next step once they can both quietly get on with their meals with just the door between them.

When the first face-to-face introduction takes place, it is wise to put a leash on both the dog and the Chausie. In all probability your cat will be interested and fairly relaxed. Once you are sure that your dog is not going to chase and isn't showing any signs of aggression, take the leash off the cat. It will help considerably if your dog is trained with basic commands such as, "Sit" and "Stay". If not, consider doing so. You can also use treats to reward your dog each time it interacts positively with your cat.

Even though the Chausie does interact well with dogs and many times will play with and even sleep curled up with a dog, keep in mind that dogs and cats can be unpredictable. Until you are 100% sure that there is harmony between them, especially if your

Chausie is still a kitten, don't leave them alone together. Even a playful bite from a dog could badly injure or even kill a kitten or a cat if the dog is large and really attacking.

If your dog is just not accepting your new cat and continues to bark and or snap at it you may have to get professional advice about how you can modify the behaviour and get your dog to calm down. Alternatively, you may have to return the cat…

Introducing your Chausie to an existing cat or cats

If there is already a resident cat in your home, expect your new Chausie to become more dominant with familiarity. It is stressful to your old pet to deal with the fact that there is another cat in the house. Quite obviously, it is stressful for you as well to make sure that your older cat does not feel neglected or out of place. You need to follow a process to make the situation more relaxed for you, your older cat and your new Chausie.

The first direct interaction should preferably be scheduled over a weekend so that you have all day to spend with the new cat and your cat-in-residence. This way, you can make sure that there are no unpleasant incidents and so that you can intervene if needs be.

It is usually best to get your older cat and new Chausie to interact during a meal time. Some growling and hissing, especially initially, is to be expected as both will want to assert themselves to some degree. However, it will not be entirely aggressive. To make sure that it does not get out of hand, though, you must place their feeding bowls at opposite ends of the room and you must stay with them. Once the feeding is done, separate them again.

Most cats are territorial by nature although your Chausie's main territory will be you. Make sure you establish the boundaries for both the cats. When your new cat is out of the confinement from its bonding or settling in room, you might want to make a special corner for him or her that is not too close to the existing space of you resident cat. Just place the feeding bowl and the cat bed in the designated area with your cat's favourite toys.

The interactions between your cats must be gradual so they become used to each other and neither feels threatened or rushed. You can try the blanket switching technique with cats so that they become more used to each other's scents or pheromones. When they are accustomed to each others' scent, they will become comfortable with each other. Increase the time they spend with each other slowly. Only when you are quite certain that they are relaxed in each other's company can you leave them alone and unsupervised. Until then you must never leave them unattended in the same space. This is especially true for night times when cats are naturally at their most active.

If you already have more than one cat at home, you will notice that one of the resident cats will take the initiative to introduce the new cat to the existing group. If this happens you are in luck as they will probably handle the situation far better than you could!

It is not uncommon for cats to not get along immediately although the Chausie gets on better with other cats far better than most other breeds. But, if your resident cat and the new kitten or cat doesn't hit it off make sure you do not punish either of them. You just need to separate them when they get anxious. You must understand that this behaviour is purely instinctive. With regular interactions, the cats will learn to live together peacefully and will decide who is who in terms of seniority or pecking order.

Your new Chausie and babies or toddlers

Chausie cats are tolerant of children and gentle with them. However, it is quite possible – and perfectly natural – that young children will get excited around a kitten or a cat. This excitement usually manifests itself as excited shouts or squeals when they first catch sight of the new kitty.

In addition to these noises that will be very loud and alarming for a new cat, a child also looks, behaves and smells very different from an adult. This unfamiliarity is distressing for the cat. There are some rules to introducing your child to the new cat that will reduce the trauma and possibility of injuries to either the cat or the child. The Chausie, however, will usually remove itself from a situation rather than becoming aggressive.

Make sure that your new cat and your child or children have regular interactions as soon as your new Chausie has started to settle and is comfortable around you. At no point should you allow the child to venture alone into the room where the new cat is still settling. You can teach your child to call and talk to the cat soothingly and even just watch the cat quietly until it gets accustomed to the child or children's presence.

It's also important to teach children not to run at or grab at a cat, as that will alarm the cat greatly as it won't understand this is a gesture of enthusiasm and affection! Children also need to be told that the cat is not a toy. You must constantly remind your child to be gentle. An enthusiastic, loving and well-intentioned hug from a toddler can result in injuries in a kitten or cat or just frighten it badly. A child needs to be taught how to hold, pick up and handle a kitten or cat and learn that pulling an ear or tail can be really painful for the cat. Also, a cat or kitten that is hurt or angry may instinctively retaliate and cause a child some pain from a scratch or a nip. If this happens, comfort your child but don't punish the cat.

Scent from hormones called pheromones are very important in the animal world. In fact, many animals relate to things purely on the basis of their smell. Cats use other senses too but scent shouldn't be underestimated. It is therefore a good idea to let your child handle some of the cat's items such as bedding or toys so that their scent is left behind for the cat to get used to. If he or she is old enough you can give your child a responsibility like handling the cat's blanket or just filling up the food or water bowl.

With much younger children like toddlers it is not realistic to give him or her responsibility for caring for the cat, but you could use the sock technique to introduce them to each other. Rub one of your toddler's socks on the cat's cheek. Then, let the toddler wear the sock. Because of this rubbing off of the scent, the cat will smell its own scent on the sock and view the toddler as a friend that he or she can trust.

Chausie cat owners all stress how tolerant and adaptable their cats are. They are very gentle and loving cats and will therefore usually make truly great companions for children to play with. In fact, children and Chausie cats often develop very close bonds.

Over and above the time you must spend getting your cat settled, introduced to the other residents, cuddling and playing with your new kitten or cat you need to start training… for both your sakes!

7) Training

While the Chausie is an intelligent cat it is still a cat. In other words, the ease with which you train a cat increases in direct proportion to the degree to which they want to be trained. In your favour, in addition to their intelligence, are the Chausie's curiosity and love of interaction, activity, stimulation and time with its owner.

Scratch Training

Getting a cat to use a scratching post rather than your furniture is usually fairly easy. Cats naturally look for a rough surface to sharpen their claws. They need to do this. You should incorporate the scratching post into play sessions in the first few days. Scratch the surface of the post with your finger nail or nails. The sound will get your kitten interested. As soon as he or she tries to catch your finger it will be introduced to a surface they like the feel of.

Continue to do this for a few days and your smart Chausie should go on using the post and leave your sofa and table legs alone. You can also use a Catnip spray on the surface of the scratching post as an added attraction. These sprays are available from pet shops and vets. Just remember to reapply the spray every three or four days as the scent fades.

32

Another option if you have a cat that keeps scratching a piece if furniture such as a sofa is to use broad packaging tape along the sections of the fabric that your cat is targeting. Cats don't like the feel or smell and this very quickly breaks them of the habit.

Litter Box Training

This is an important area of training, as nobody wants a cat that is not housetrained. In this regard you will be assisted by the intelligence of the Chausie and the inherently fastidious and clean feline nature.

Keep in mind that a kitten is a baby. Like human babies it will be busy playing or doing something and not realize till the last minute that it needs to urinate or defecate. For this reason you need to expect the odd accident and be sensible about where you place the litter box. Your kitten will sometimes need to get to it in a hurry.

The best places to put a litter box are away from areas where the cat eats, where food is stored or prepared and in a quite place (cats like privacy too). A corner is also usually ideal. If your house is large or has more than one level, it can be a good idea to have more than one litter box. Also, if you have more than one cat, you will need more than one box because cats don't like to share. Finally, don't move the litter box around so that your kitten or cat knows where to find it.

It is very important to show your kitten where the litter box is. One needs to establish a routine:

- ✓ Place your kitten gently into the litter box a few minutes after a meal and after he or she wakes up
- ✓ Be patient. Give your kitten time to walk around and sniff the litter box
- ✓ The instinct to dig and bury waste usually emerges on its own. If it doesn't, gently take a front paw and show him or her how to dig and scratch in the sand. Alternatively, dig a little hole in the (clean) litter with your fingers

33

- ✓ Every time your Chausie kitten uses the litter box give it lots of praise and cuddles
- ✓ Don't ever shout at or otherwise frighten a kitten in a litter box because he or she will make a negative association.

Furthermore, if you are spending time with your kitten and watching it you will notice the signs that it needs to use the box. Don't rush at or alarm it; gently pick it up and place it in the litter tray.

Once the litter box has been used the likelihood that the kitten will return increases as his or her scent has been left behind. In the event of an accident – and these will happen – you can take some of the waste and place it in the box as this might help to increase the scent levels and strengthen the association.

And don't ever shout at or hit a kitten that has had an accident. It won't know what you are angry about and will begin to fear you or feel nervous instead of understanding why you are upset or angry. It is far better if you praise good behaviour – the use of the litter box – and intervene when you see an accident is imminent in order to re-enforce the connection.

In order to encourage your kitten to make the transition from litter box to outdoor area or garden, you just need to slowly move the litter box closer and closer to the external door that the kitten or the cat will use. Eventually you will move the litter box to just outside the door. When you see your kitten or cat in the litter box and about to use it, pick it up gently and show it a suitable patch of earth that is soft enough to dig in. In time he or she will pick their favourite spots.

Toilet Training

Most of us are happy to teach our kittens to use a litter box and then gradually teach them to use the garden or an outside area. There are, however, some cat owners who want their cat to use

34

the toilet. The nature of the Chausie will help with this more complex training, especially if it's disguised as a game.

The first step is to place the litter box on the floor, right next to the toilet, for a few days. Thereafter you will need to gradually raise the litter box until it is at the same height as the toilet seat. At the same time as raising the box, you need to gradually decrease the amount of litter in it.

The next stage in the process involves moving the box onto the toilet seat in 1" (2.5cm) increments. Eventually the box will be directly over the seat and there should only be a very thin layer of litter left in it.

At this point the litter box is replaced with a training box. You have two options: a commercially available product or a homemade one. If you opt for the latter you can fasten wax paper, plastic or (aluminium) foil over the toilet bowl, under the seat. Sprinkle a handful of litter onto the training box.

A word of caution: make sure whatever material you use is strong enough to hold the weight of the kitten or cat when it steps onto it or jumps up. If he or she falls in the toilet that's it; you can forget toilet training!

The next stage is to cut a hole that is 1" (2.5cm) in diameter in the material you have used. Gradually increase the diameter until the material is almost cut back right to the bowl. At this stage of the training the sprinkling of litter has gone entirely.

Finally, remove the training box or seat entirely. Don't teach your Chausie to flush; they can enjoy it so much it will drive you nuts and waste a lot of water! You will have to flush the toilet yourself.

Swimming pools

Many Chausies, perhaps thanks to their Jungle Cat roots, love water. However, because they are happy to go into water and enjoy being in it doesn't mean that they can climb out of a swimming pool with ease and that is the danger.

It is therefore very important that you show your cat where to get out of the water and give it enough practice in doing so that he or she will be able to get itself out of the water without difficulty even if you are not there to help.

Doing tricks

Some feel that cats shouldn't be trained to do tricks because it is somehow beneath their dignity. This is a very personal choice. Actually it will probably be your cat's decision rather than yours; some cats are just not interested. Your Chausie, though, is likely to be an enthusiastic pupil. There is no doubt that the intelligence and instincts found in these cats mean that you can train them to do tricks far more easily than many breeds.

There are numerous instances of cats that play fetch and the Chausie is one of the breeds that loves this game. As with any behaviour you want to reinforce and encourage, rewards are very important as motivators for your cat. With a Chausie the treat doesn't have to be edible because your cat will be addicted to time with you and attention from you.

Some cats also sit on command. This can be achieved by holding a treat above the cat's head and saying, "Sit!" If he or she does, hand over the treat. If not, repeat the command while gently but firmly pushing the cat's bottom down and then giving a treat. Keep this routine up until the cat sits when asked to.

Agility training

Agility training is something you can do with your Chausie just because it is fun for both of you rather than because you want to enter or compete in agility shows or contests. It is also a wonderful way to exercise an active, athletic cat, especially an indoor one.

Your Chausie will be ideal for agility activities for several reasons. Firstly, these are intelligent cats that thrive on new activities, stimulation and challenges. Secondly, they are easy to train thanks to both their intelligence and enthusiasm. Finally, your cat will love playing and having one-on-one time with you.

You don't need special equipment for agility training. You can use things around the house to set up an agility course that provides things to jump or climb over and tunnels to run through. A paper bag cut open at both ends makes good a tunnel. A wooden, long handled utensil such as a spoon balanced on top of two mugs or rolls of toilet paper will make a perfectly good hurdle.

Of course you can buy equipment from a supplier. Either way, remember that you must build an agility course that should be like a playground for your cat. Keep your cat's age and size in mind so you don't expect too much or push too hard. It must be fun for both of you.

You can start agility training when a kitten is really young. Just be patient and gentle and stop when your kitty shows signs of being tired or losing interest. Remember this is supposed to be fun, not military boot camp! Don't ever force your cat to do anything. If your cat seems tired or indicates it has had enough, give your Chausie a rest and try again later or the next day. It is important, though, to do these agility activities with your cat every day.

Using a toy of some kind that will grab your kitten or cat's attention and lure it through a tunnel or hoop or over an obstacle is a very effective training tool. There are cat toys with feathers on them that are not too expensive and are ideal for this purpose. Wiggle the toy at the end of the tunnel or other side of an obstacle to entice your cat through or over it. A cat's natural desire to chase and pounce will work with you.

As with any training, treats should be used to reward the cat each time it does something correctly or well. You can also use a clicker bought from a vet store. Clicker training means that when your cat gets it right you 'click' and give it a treat. Do not forget the treat must be accompanied by verbal praise and cuddles.

8) How long a Chausie can be left alone

Chausies do not like being left alone at all. If you can't be there you need to provide an animal companion, either another cat or a cat-friendly dog, so that the Chausie has companionship.

A cat that is left alone often and for extended periods will become stressed, unhappy and may even become destructive from both unhappiness and sheer boredom.

9) Transporting your Chausie

Much of this is really common sense... Never drive or travel in a car with a cat sitting on your lap or on the back or the front seat. The cat could very easily become frightened, jump onto the driver or get under the driver's feet and cause an accident.

Use a carry cage or basket to contain the cat. Do not use a cardboard box as the cat may escape or claw its way out if it is very frightened. If you must leave your cat in the car on a hot day, make sure that the car is parked in a cool, shaded spot and that the windows are down slightly to allow some airflow.

Before leaving on a long journey, restrict the cat's food and water intake for 2 to 3 hours. In hot weather, the cat will need to have a drink now and then throughout the day.

10) To microchip your cat or not

The reason to micro-chip an animal is to help to trace it if it is lost. A microchip is one aspect of cat identification. The other is a break-away collar with a disc. Although a chip can be effective, it is not fool-proof. The down side is that having a chip will only help if someone takes your cat to a shelter if it gets lost. Also, while most animal shelters have scanners and use them, this is not true of all of them. This is why also having a collar and tag is a good idea.

The procedure is fairly simple and should, preferably, be done by a vet. A large needle is used to place the chip, which is about the size of a grain of rice, under the skin, between the cat's shoulder blades. A special scanner can read the unique number on the chip. The procedure only takes a few seconds and the sensation is the same as having blood drawn. In other words, there is a little pain and discomfort but it is very brief.

There is an extremely small possibility of complications happening after the chip implant. For instance, a few animals have developed tumours at the site where the chip was placed. This is, however, statistically very unlikely.

The cost of micro-chipping at time of writing is in the region of $50 in America and up to £40 in the UK depending on when it's done and who does it. If you are going to have this procedure done, you can take your cat in to the vet from the age of 12 weeks onwards.

The chips used in different parts of the world also utilize different frequencies. The UK and Europe use a 134.2 kilohertz chip while a 125 and 128 kilohertz chip is used in America. If you are going to take your cat across a border you should check in advance on the requirements as some countries have regulations about both chip date and type.

Chapter 7: Feeding your Chausie

1) What to feed your kitten and how often

A kitten's nutritional needs and digestive capabilities are not the same as those of an adult cat. For the first year of your cat's life you will need to give it a balanced diet using a good quality kitten food that you can purchase either from your vet or a pet shop. If you are unsure what brand to buy, ask your vet for advice.

If you decide you want to feed your young Chausie raw meat you must keep in mind that this diet won't provide all the nutrition and trace elements that a growing cat needs. As a result you will also need to give your kitty a nutritional supplement. The bottom line is that the nutrition a kitten gets will lay the foundations for future health!

2) What to feed adult cats and how often

Thanks to their 'wild' ancestors, some Chausies have shorter than usual intestines. This is especially true of first and second generation cats. This leads to their systems being less able to cope with poor quality cat foods.

In some cases, inferior foods could lead to the cat developing food allergies and chronic intestinal inflammation causing weight loss, pain, vomiting and diarrhea. If this happens a vet must be involved.

The foods that affected Chausies can't tolerate contain cereals, herbs or spices and other plant or plant-based materials. This means that this breed does best on a diet of meat, offal, digestible bone, or a premium commercial food that a reputable breeder or a vet recommends. You should also ensure, though, that a diet of meat and bones does provide your cat with all the nutrients that are essential for its health.

Standard foods and diet

Eating canned cat food every day is not recommended. Many cat owners feel that canned food once or twice a week is more than adequate.

Also keep in mind that some canned foods are better than others. It's important to read the label on the tin to ensure that the contents do not contain sugar or inferior meats. Specifically look for canned foods that list meat or chicken as the first or second ingredient. Your cat's food should be served at room temperature.

Just like people, cats like variety in their diet. If you decide to change your cat's diet you need to do so gradually. Keep an eye on your cat and if there is any evidence of gastric problems you need to reconsider the food your Chausie is being given.

Dry food is a healthy option for your cat. Not only does it provide nutrition it may also help to keep your cat's teeth clean and its gums healthy if you get a correctly formulated food. Investing in a food dispenser is a good idea as it means that your cat can snack even when you are not around, day or night.

Just keep in mind that a cat that is eating more dry food will need to drink a lot of water. There must always be a good supply of fresh clean water available for you kitten or cat! Either there must be a bowl of water or you could invest in a more sophisticated option: a cat's drinking fountain.

Chausies love food and are keen to try anything. A word of warning, though: do *not* give your cat human's food! This applies to scraps when you are cooking, treats from your plate during meals or leftovers. Firstly, your cat may be exposed to food stuffs that are toxic for him or her. Secondly, your cat will put on weight. Furthermore, you will end up with a cat that begs or even steals food.

As mentioned, some Chausie owners believe very strongly in a diet that consists only of raw food and bones. Proponents of this

41

diet state that their cats are healthier overall. Others think that any balanced, varied diet will be healthy. Yet other cat lovers believe that foods containing grains should be avoided. Again, when in doubt your best advisors will be the breeder your cat came from or your vet.

Giving your cat small portions regularly helps it to control body heat, protects its digestive systems and lessens the risk of it becoming overweight.

Preventative nutrition

Let's talk now about "preventative nutrition" which is the best kind of nutrition for your cat. If you think that your cat is "fine" and continue to give it foods that are not really recommended, there is a chance that it will at some stage develop serious health issues. For instance, cats that are constantly and exclusively given dry foods can suddenly develop the following conditions:

- Inflammatory Bowel Disease
- Asthma due to allergens
- Inflamed bladder
- Blocked urinary tract that, if severe, can led to rupture of the bladder and death
- Feline Diabetes
- Kidney stones.

These conditions can be prevented with a little attention to the food that your kitten and later your cat is given. As a pet owner, it is your responsibility to choose a diet that ensures longevity and long term health benefits for your Chausie. In order to understand preventive nutrition, here are some things that you must learn about the nutritional requirements in cats.

Firstly, carbohydrates are very damaging to a cat's health. They cause diabetes, which is one of the most common diseases in domesticated cats these days. Cats are carnivores by design and nature, so feeding them on carbohydrates or plant-based proteins will upset their digestive system and potentially lead to more serious conditions or problems. This is, because of the length of the intestinal tract, especially true of the Chausie.

Secondly, the thirst drive is low in cats. It is therefore necessary for them to drink water along with their food. In the wild, the food that cats eat consists of almost 75% of water. Domestic cats will never make up for the lack of water by lapping from their water bowls. Water is extremely important to keep your cat healthy. If the cat's body does not receive the necessary amount of water there may be harmful repercussions such as urinary tract obstructions and / or infections. These problems are not common in cats that normally consume canned foods or other forms of wet food.

In addition, there are no benefits to the dental health of your cat from standard dry foods. There are some foods that have been specially developed by a manufacturer for cat's and their dental needs. These special – and sometimes expensive – foods are available from a vet.

However, there are some experts who claim that these foods that supposedly promote dental health don't actually work either because, although several dry food companies may claim this, there is no clear scientific basis to prove that this is true for cats. If you are unsure, approach a cat association or a third party whose only concern is cat's welfare.

In short, preventive nutrition is the only way to ensure that your Chausie has long lasting benefits from the food that it consumes. Not all pet owners understand the principle that preventive nutrition is based upon. With reference to the understanding that you have acquired from the points mentioned above, here are the five principles of preventive nutrition that you can follow to ensure optimized and holistic nutrition for your cat:

✓ There must always be fresh water available
✓ Your cat needs to snack a great deal so food must always be available
✓ Provide a mixture of dry and wet or canned food

✓ Avoid foods that contain grains and carbohydrates
✓ Provide a balanced diet that is not too high in proteins or fats
✓ Ensure your cat is getting the vitamins and minerals it needs.

Food formulated by experts

Creating the right food for cats is not easy. There is a certain amount of expertise that is very important to ensure that all the key ingredients and nutrients are present in the formulae. There are specialized pet nutritionists who work to provide your cat with an optimized formula to ensure the correct nutrition. These foods are tested and tried for their effects before they are released for pet owners to use for their cats. There are several feeding trials that are conducted to understand how effective the formula is in enhancing the health of your cat.

According to association officials in America, feeding trials are the most important tools to understand the quality of a pet food. Those that have undergone feeding trials are given to the pets under recommended guidelines, which must be strictly followed to make sure that the cats get the right nutrition from them.

The quality controls involved in the development and testing of these foods begins with the concern with safety. There are several manufacturers that produce these foods in their own facilities and they are, generally, thought to be more trustworthy for a few reasons.

Firstly, the quality control is better as the source of the ingredients and all the associated processes are monitored effectively. All the foods that are manufactured on site are held until they meet all the safety guidelines recommended for the product. As a result, issues like Salmonella contamination are effectively prevented.

In addition, when you purchase a certain cat food, check if the food has been 'manufactured by' or just has been 'distributed by' the brand that you are choosing. If the brand that you are purchasing is made and distributed by the same company, it is easier to register complaints with respect to the quality of the food provided. You can report all the concerns that you have on the quality of the food to the manufacturer directly.

There are several brands and types of cat foods available and they are formulated for cats of various activity levels, ages and breeds. Some also help to prevent certain problems such as hairball formation.

There are several "life stage foods" that have been formulated because the nutritional requirements vary from kittens to adult and senior cats. However, there is another variety called the "ALL life stage" food that is available in some countries. This is definitely not widely recommended as it may lead to malnutrition or even excessive nutrition which could lead to several serious health issues in your cat.

If you find it hard to make a decision with regards to the right food choice for your feline friend, ask for help or advice from your vet or pet store salesperson. He or she should be able to help based on the breed and age of your cat.

3) What not to feed your Chausie cat

Usually cat owners think that their pets instinctively know what is best for them. Cats can be picky eaters but there is little evidence that suggests that a cat knows what is right for it and what is wrong. Perhaps in the wild cats follow their instincts and get the right nutrition. However, with domesticated cats the varieties of foods that are available will make them interested in all the wrong sorts of things.

There are a number of food stuffs that should not be given to your Chausie or any cat for that matter:

- Onions, chives and garlic: at best your kitty's digestive system will be unhappy. At worst, eating onion regularly or a large amount can lead to anaemia.

- Milk and other dairy products: despite the clichés such as, "You look like the cat that ate the cream" and images of cats lapping milk, most cats are lactose intolerant.
- Caffeine: this can be fatal for cats. There is caffeine in tea, cocoa, carbonated drinks, many energy drinks and some cough and cold remedies. It is not only found in coffee.
- Chocolate: it contains theobromine which is highly toxic for cats and can lead to death. The darker the chocolate the more poisonous it is for cats.
- Liver: kittens especially shouldn't be fed liver as it is high in vitamin A. Too much of the vitamin can lead to severe bone problems and malformations.
- Raisins and grapes: for reasons that are still unclear, these can lead to kidney failure.
- Sweets/candy, diet foods and drinks, baked goods and some toothpaste: some of these contain the sugar substitute Xylitol, which can cause liver failure in cats.
- Raw eggs: avidin, the protein in the egg white, inhibits the absorption of biotin, a vitamin necessary for skin health.
- Alcohol (yes, some – who don't deserve a pet – think it's funny to get a pet drunk): it has the same effect on a cat's brain and liver as it does on ours. The difference is that 3 teaspoons of whiskey will kill a 5lb or 2.3kg cat.
- Yeast dough: uncooked dough is never recommended for a cat. If your cat eats dough there is a chance that it will actually begin to rise inside the cat's stomach. During this expansion, the dough may stretch the stomach and abdomen causing pain or internal injury. In addition, the cat may suffer alcohol poisoning as the yeast ferments.
- Dog food: A bite once in a while will not harm your cat too much. However, the formula used in dog food is obviously for dogs and therefore definitely not suitable for cats. Cat food is packed with the proteins and vitamins necessary to fulfil a cat's nutritional requirements. On the other hand, dog foods may contain plant proteins that are not suitable for cats. If your Chausie regularly consumes dog food, it might become malnourished.

Often, being cautious isn't enough and your cat might make its way into your kitchen or pantry and have a generous helping of restricted foods. There is no need to be unduly alarmed. Find out what it is that your cat has eaten and, in most cases, your vet will be able to provide an antidote to take care of the situation for you.

The golden rule is to stick to food and treats formulated for cats. No matter how much you think of your Chausie as a person, he or she is a cat. And be careful about what you leave within easy reach of your cat.

4) Treats

Treats are both a way of saying you love your cat and of rewarding good or desirable behaviour. While praise or a cuddle from you is probably what your Chausie likes the most, treats are also very useful.

Using treats as part of an exercise routine can work, especially if you live in a smaller home or your cat is purely an indoor cat. You could hide a couple of dry treats around the house each day and your cat will get some exercise finding them. It is a good idea to start this routine when your Chausie is still young.

If you are unsure what treats are healthy for your cat, purchase them directly from your vet or you could ask the staff there for recommendations or suggestions. An alternative is to make your own treats by cooking up a little meat or chicken and giving your cat a small piece at a time.

Treats also don't have to be in edible form. What about a fun toy or some catnip?

Chapter 8: Grooming your Chausie

The Chausie is a very low maintenance breed when it comes to grooming. A weekly brushing will keep its coat free of dead and loose hair. Helping your cat get rid of dead hair becomes more important during the times the seasons change, especially during spring, as shedding increases greatly.

You need to help your cat avoid ingesting too much hair when he or she grooms and you don't want to have fur-covered furniture, bedding, etc.

1) Bathing your Chausie

With this breed a bath should not be necessary. However, if your cat somehow gets really dirty and needs to be bathed you must use a shampoo that is suitable for cats. Fortunately the Chausie usually rather enjoys having a bath.

You need to get a number of things ready before you fetch your kitten or cat. You need to run warm or body temperature, *not* hot, water into the bathtub, basin, sink or container. The water should be body temperature or your cat may develop dandruff. As the water runs, add a small amount of shampoo to the water. Also, put a clean towel close by. Truly adoring cat owners will warm the towel slightly! Putting your cat into a bath or shower with you is not recommended.

Place your Chausie gently into the water and wet him or her using a cup, small jug or some other suitable container. Once your cat is wet it is time for the shampoo. As with any animal, try not to get shampoo in your cat's eyes.

Once you have rinsed off all the shampoo with clean water, lift your cat out and wrap it in a towel. Talk soothingly to your cat throughout the bath. Ending the bath and with a treat in addition to praise and affection is a good idea!

2) *Nail care and clipping*

If you need to trim your cat's nails, use a small pair of fingernail clippers. Cut with care so as not to nick the skin or flesh around the nails. If your Chausie is a wriggler you must enlist help so that injuries are avoided.

3) *Ear care*

Use a cat-safe, gentle cleaning solution and good quality ear buds or Q-tips so that you don't deposit fibres and threads as you remove dirt. Warning: don't put the Q-tip or ear bud too deep into the ear as you will damage it and cause a great deal of pain.

4) *Tooth care*

Tooth or dental care is discussed fully in chapter 9 as it is a very important aspect of grooming and protecting the overall health and well-being of your cat.

5) *Products to use*

As with cat litter and food, there is a wide choice when it comes to cat-specific bath, cleaning or hygiene products. If you are unsure about what would be best, be guided by a breeder or by your vet when it comes to the best shampoo and so on.

The other items you will use are ones that people use too: ear buds or Q-tips, cotton wipes or swabs, mild baby wipes and fingernail clippers. Just be sure to buy good quality and hypoallergenic items.

Chapter 9: Your Chausie's health

The Chausie is generally a very robust and healthy breed, although some cats may suffer from genetic illnesses.

1) Finding a good vet

It is necessary for you to have a reliable vet who you can trust with your pet. It is never a good idea to constantly change the vet who treats your Chausie. Cats can find change difficult and most animals are reluctant to co-operate with vets. So, you must give your cat time to get accustomed to the scent, touch and voice of one vet.

Once your cat is comfortable with him or her, it will be more relaxed during visits to the vet. A vet is an important part of your cat's life and you must make sure you look for the perfect one to take care of your pet.

There will in all probability be several large and small veterinary clinics around your town or city area. As a result, there can be a huge choice which can be confusing rather than helpful when you set out to choose one for your Chausie. The best way to look for a vet is to ask for recommendations from the breeder and your cat-owning friends and neighbours.

You must make an effort to look for someone who specializes in cat care. Alternatively, you can go to a vet practice that does at least have one or two vets who work mainly with cats. There are a few aspects that you might want to consider before you decide on a vet:

o   How far is the vet from your home?
o   Is the commuting time too long in event of an emergency?
o   Do you like the staff and find them confidence inspiring?

It is always better to find someone close to your house. It should preferably not take more than 15 minutes to drive down to your vet. Once you have found someone who seems to fit into all the requirements, you can make a trial visit. The chemistry between your cat and the vet is extremely important if you want to make it a long-lasting relationship.

There are some signs that will indicate how comfortable you and your pet will be in a particular clinic. Make the following observations when you are visiting the vet for the first time.

- The waiting room must be clean and well maintained
- The ambience must be comforting for the cat so that it feels secure when it is being examined
- If it is a common clinic for dogs and cats, how are they housed when they are admitted for hospital care?
- The people at the reception must be friendly and helpful. They are going to be your point of contact in the coming sessions and you must be comfortable with them.

Once you are in the examination room, check how the vet interacts with both the animals and their owners. His or her tone must be soothing. The vet should be able to provide undivided attention to the animal being examined. He or she must also value your opinions about your cat's health, be willing to answer your questions and explain the situation with your cat, and must be respectful towards you and your feelings.

The personality of your vet plays an important part in the way he or she interacts with the animals being examined and treated. A vet must be genuinely passionate about his or her job. Without passion, you cannot be assured that a vet will go to all lengths to ensure the best for your Chausie.

The vet you select must be good with cats and have a complete and up to date knowledge of the different practices and techniques that have been developed in veterinary practice. He or she must also make a conscious effort to upgrade his or her skills and knowledge.

Once you are reassured about the behaviour of the vet towards you and your cat, you need to get down to the technical and legal aspects of choosing a vet.

- ✓ Is the facility equipped to handle emergencies?
- ✓ How many cages or rooms do they have for the pets that have been admitted?
- ✓ Are dogs and cats housed together?
- ✓ Is every staff member appropriately educated or trained?
- ✓ Is the facility licensed?
- ✓ What are the costs for tests and surgeries?
- ✓ Is the pricing competitive enough?
- ✓ What insurance policies do they accept?
- ✓ Are emergencies handled after regular working hours?
- ✓ Who takes care of the pets when they are hospitalized?
- ✓ Are they open to alternative medicines and treatments?
- ✓ Are there billing and administration systems reliable and accurate?

Once you've received satisfactory answers to all these questions, you can be assured that this facility is best suited for your cat. Remember, the person you choose as your vet is going to be your partner in the wellbeing of your Chausie for many years to come.

2) Preparing your cat for a vet visit

Taking a cat to the vet is not easy... for either of you! As a result, it is best that you prepare your cat well for a visit to the vet. Here are five tips that will make the visit less stressful for your cat:

The pre vet visit routine

Cats require a good amount of mental preparation before they are taken to the vet.

Start by giving your Chausie a thorough check up from head to toe. This is a more relaxed imitation of the examination that will take place in the vet's clinic. The idea is to get the cat used to being handled by the vet. Obviously in the event of an emergency this kind of preparation can't happen as there is no time.

Getting your cat used to the carrier is another way to making the visit less stressful. If your cat learns to associate the carrier with vet visits only, it might start to resist and fight being put into the carrier. On the other hand, if you create associations like play time or even outdoor visits with the carrier, your Chausie might look forward to the positive activities and be less stressed. You can also designate the carrier as a nap place. Throw in your cat's favourite toys and treats inside the carrier to attract it towards it.

The actual drive to the vet is not going to create as much stress in your Chausie as in most cats because they usually enjoy the car. However, if he or she is a bit anxious you can reduce this by talking soothingly to him or her and, if possible, placing the carrier in such a way that your cat can see you.

Make your car cat friendly

If you have an atypical Chausie that doesn't enjoy a trip in the car and is frightened by the noise and the smell you can help your cat make positive associations by including drives in the car in your daily or at least weekly routine. You can take the car for short distances too. Take the car to the park, for instance. Then your Chausie will stop making negative associations. You can even stop by at the vet's clinic for 5 minutes to get your cat used to the staff there.

The basic idea is to get your cat used to the car. He or she must learn to be calm and relaxed during these visits. Keeping some toys in car and allowing your Chausie to play during these drives will also help.

Dealing with the waiting room

One place dreaded by all animals is the waiting room at the clinic. There are several unpleasant sounds like the barking of dogs, cats wailing and even chatter of humans that increase the levels of anxiety in a cat. There are also a lot of scary and unpleasant scents: dogs, other cats, unknown people, antiseptic, disinfectant and do on.

Cats are, by nature, solitary animals when they are not feeling well. Cats, regardless of whether they are well, sick, relaxed or stressed don't like being introduced to so many strange sights and sounds at one go. In addition, your Chausie is a very sensitive, intuitive cat that will pick up fear in the other animals there. Animals can also discern ill health and pain in each other. The best thing to do would be to leave your cat in the carrier till he is called in for examination. This gives him a secure hide-out and he or she will be less anxious or frightened.

Make sure that the carrier you are using is large enough. Place a nice cat bed or a cushion inside for him or her to rest on. You can also leave toys and goodies inside the carrier. A top loading carrier is a must as it will become difficult or even impossible for you to get your frightened kitty out of a front loading one.

Special pheromone sprays are available to reduce anxiety and stress in cats during their visit to the vet. These sprays imitate the scent that cats leave when they rub themselves against the legs of their loved ones.

You can also schedule your more routine appointments to the less busy parts of the day. That way, the chaos in the waiting room will be reduced, making your cat feel more relaxed.

Get friendly with your vet

It is good to allow your vet to spend some time with your cat and break the ice. A good vet will take a few minutes to soothe a cat patient, and will give your Chausie a chance to sniff his or her coat and hands, for example.

Of course, the vet is going to have to poke and prod the cat during the examination. However, this becomes less stressful if the cat can look at the vet as a friend rather a stranger. Make sure you clear up all queries related to your cat's wellbeing when you visit your vet.

Send items from home

If your cat is scheduled for overnight hospital care or going to be admitted as a result of illness or injury, it can help if you send its favourite items from home, for example a blanket and a toy. The idea is to keep him or her around familiar scents as this should reduce anxiety levels. There will, however, be times the vet won't allow this as items from home will not be sterile.

Visits from you if your cat will be at the vet for an extended period may or may not reduce your cat's stress and anxiety levels. Your cat may just become distressed when you leave without him or her and confused about what is happening. Your vet will advise you about this.

You must always work with you vet to ensure the complete well-being of your cat. You must be able to trust the knowledge and expertise of your vet if you want him or her to be the best care-giver for your cat. Usually vets will be more than willing to lend support in the form of information or study material to help you understand how you can best take care of your cat at home.

3) Vaccinations

There is a range of vaccines for cats. They are placed into two groups: core and noncore.

The core vaccines protect against rabies, distemper, feline viral rhinotracheitis and feline calicivirus. These vaccines are given approximately every 3 years but more often in high risk areas. As with so much else, your vet will be your best guide.

Noncore vaccines are used based on a variety of factors such as breed, age, health status, the risk of exposure to certain diseases and how common a disease is in that area. In many instances cat associations recommend against these vaccines, such as FeLV for feline leukaemia. This is especially true for indoor cats.

The core vaccination timetable is:

> ➤ 6 – 7 weeks: Combination vaccine
> ➤ 10 weeks: Combination vaccine (distemper, rhinotracheitis and calicivirus) and Chlamydophila if necessary
> ➤ 12 weeks and older (governed by local laws): Rabies
> ➤ 13 weeks: Combination vaccine (distemper, rhinotracheitis and calicivirus) and Chlamydophila and Feline Leukaemia if the kitten is at risk of exposure.
> ➤ 16 and 19 weeks: Combination vaccine (distemper, rhinotracheitis, and calicivirus) and Feline Leukaemia if the kitten is at risk of exposure
> ➤ Adult cats: Combination vaccine (distemper, rhinotracheitis and calicivirus) and Chlamydophila and Feline Leukaemia if the cat is at risk of exposure.

If you acquired your kitten from a breeder the initial vaccinations will already have been done. It is vital that you keep up with them, particularly if your cat will be exposed to other cats or you live in a high risk area.

4) Neutering and spaying

As far as many are concerned, unless you are planning to breed with your Chausie you should have your cat spayed or neutered as soon as it is old enough.

Spaying is the surgical removal of the ovaries and uterus of a female cat. Neutering or castration is the surgical removal of the testicles from male cats. The hospitalization is brief, recovery is quick and the health and behavioural benefits last a lifetime!

The advantages for female cats are that they are far less likely to get breast cancer and will of course not contract uterine infections. In addition, they will no longer go into heat and indulge in activities like urinating and yowling to attract mates. This will help your pocket and your home.

With male cats, neutering prevents testicular cancer and means that your cat is far less likely to roam and therefore less likely to get into fights with other cats, be attacked by dogs or hit by a car.

In addition, the world has enough unwanted, homeless kittens. You don't want to have to home kittens that your Chausie cat produced after a minute of fun with the cat next door! Pet owners must take responsibility for the reproductive behaviour of their pets.

To bust other myths, spaying and neutering will not make your cat fat, frustrated, crazed or depressed. Having this done is good for the cat, for you and for the community.

Best time for spaying

This breed enters puberty fairly late and does not reach maturity until around two years of age. Your vet will advise you on the best age at which to have the sterilization done so that your cat's health is not compromised. Sterilising an animal that is too young can create problems, especially for male cats.

To reduce the chances of aggression and also pregnancies, make sure you schedule to have your Chausie spayed or neutered before it begins to mark its territory. This is when you know that your cat is physically ready to find a mate. It you have a female cat at home you must have her spayed to avoid any chance of her becoming pregnant.

In case you have neglected spaying or neutering, you can even take your cat to the vet when she is in heat. However, this can lead to excessive blood loss, which is certainly not desirable. If you think that you want your adult cat to be neutered or spayed, you can consult your vet about the safety of the procedure.

Behaviour changes after neutering or spaying

There is no apparent permanent change in a cat's personality after neutering or spaying. It is true that the cat might be quiet and subdued and not too playful for a while but he or she will get back to their usual self as soon as he or she recovers from the procedure. You may have to provide your cat with a certain diet after neutering or spaying. This is to ensure that the cat gets all the nutrients and calories required during the recovery process. If you have any concerns about the process of neutering or spaying, your vet will be able to provide you with all the necessary details.

5) General early signs of illness

Naturally the sooner you realise that your Chausie is not well the better as your cat will suffer less and treatment is more likely to be effective.

As you get to know your Chausie it will become increasingly easy for you to see when he or she is not well. Don't be concerned if your cat seems little off-colour for a day because that's fairly normal, but if the symptoms persist for two more days then you need to take action. Obviously if the symptoms are dramatic or severe or your cat has suffered an injury you need to take it to the vet immediately!

Behavioural changes to watch out for because they can be very good indicators of poor health include:

> ➤ Marked and sudden increase or decrease in appetite
> ➤ Extreme tiredness or lethargy
> ➤ Difficulty in standing or moving around
> ➤ Drinking far more water than usual
> ➤ Swelling of any part of the body or bloating of the abdomen
> ➤ Atypical behaviour such as aggression
> ➤ Difficulty with defecation or urination or the opposite (incontinence)

➢ Discharge from the nose, ears, eyes or any other body opening
➢ Excessive licking, scratching or biting at a part of the body.

Signs that your Chausie is in pain include crying, tilting or shaking their head in the event of ear pain, constant licking, limping dragging a limb, crying or even a hissing if the painful area is touched, rubbing or pawing at an eye, and mouth pain may cause increased salivation.

6) Common cat illnesses and health problems

Vomiting

Vomiting is a very common feline disorder. Usually cats vomit when they consume something that disagrees with them, is poisonous to some degree or an object that is not digestible. In addition to these situations, it can also be a symptom of some form of infection, diabetes or even a urinary tract disease.

Feline lower urinary tract infection

Almost 10% of cats get affected at same stage in their lives by feline lower urinary tract infections. There are multiple causes for this group of disorders that affects both male and female cats. Most often it is stress related. In other cases, cats that eat fried foods might suffer from this condition. Feline lower urinary tract disorders are especially common in cats that are generally unhealthy, overweight or getting elderly.

The symptoms for feline lower urinary tract disorder include:

- The cat strains when urinating
- There are traces of blood in the urine
- The cat urinates in unusual places
- Loud purrs or cries while urinating
- Constant licking in the urinary area to reduce the pain
- Depression
- Sudden Dehydration

- Loss of appetite
- Constant vomiting.

The treatment for feline lower urinary tract infection depends on the cause and the type and degree of infection. The inability to urinate is a matter of great concern in pets. You must call your vet immediately if you observe one or more of the above symptoms.

Tapeworms

An internal infestation by tapeworms can be hazardous to your cat's health. These parasites usually invade the intestines of cats and can grow up to 2 feet in length if left untreated. Tapeworm infections have very subtle symptoms. This is why you must always keep a close watch on your cat to ensure that the problem of tapeworms does not go undetected. The symptoms include sudden weight loss even though the cat is eating, chronic vomiting and the presence of small white worms in the faeces and in the anal region.

The last symptom is an almost certain indication that a cat really is infected by tapeworms. This problem is usually linked with the presence of fleas on a cat because ingesting a flea can result in an infection by tapeworms. It is important to handle fleas as well when you are tackling the issue of tapeworms. The most common modes of treatment include tropical medication, oral medicines and injections.

Remember, too, that people can pick up tapeworms that can lead to infestations and even severe complications. Use a scoop or gloves when cleaning a cat box and wash your hands thoroughly.

Diarrhoea

Just as with other gastric upsets, there are several possible reasons for cats to develop diarrhoea. They range from those that are not a cause for real concern to serious conditions. The most common causes include a diet that is too rich, eating spoiled food, liver disease, allergies or food sensitivity such as lactose intolerance or cancer.

The biggest problem with diarrhoea is the danger of dehydration. It is therefore essential to give your cat plenty of fresh, clean water to drink to prevent this. Dehydration can lead to kidney and other complications that can be fatal if left untreated for too long. You must also reduce the quantity of food you give to your Chausie for about 24 hours.

If the diarrhoea continues and is accompanied by a loss of appetite, lethargy, bloody stools and a fever you must take your cat to the vet as a matter of urgency for examination, diagnosis and suitable treatment.

Constipation

This is the most common digestive problem in domestic cats. A healthy cat will have a single, normal bowel movement a day. If your cat is constipated there is either a problem with its diet or there could be a more serious underlying health problem. Chausie cats that are more prone to constipation include overweight cats, elderly cats and those that have a low fibre diet and insufficient exercise.

Signs to watch out for include straining and crying when eliminating or trying to do so; small, dry and hard stools; stools that are covered in mucous or blood; frequent and unproductive trips to the litter box; loss of appetite; vomiting; weight loss; lethargy; signs of abdominal discomfort such as constant licking of their tummy; and a lack of general grooming. These are all indicators of serious constipation and you need to consult a vet.

The causes of constipation include factors such as dehydration or insufficient fibre in the diet, an enlarged prostate gland in male cats, a blockage or abscess in the anal sacs, a side effect of a medication, a tumour or other obstruction in the intestine, an abnormality in the colon itself, diabetes, a hernia, obesity or a foreign object the cat swallowed that is causing a blockage.

Treatment will of course be determined by the cause of the cat's constipation. However, there are a number of stool softening and laxative products available for cats that are usually effective and easy to administer. Your vet may recommend a high-fibre diet for your Chausie and / or an increase in water consumption and in exercise. Avoid using liquid or medicinal paraffin.

In very severe cases a vet may have to perform an enema to flush out the colon or even perform a manual evacuation of the bowels. In the event of a tumour, hernia, obstruction or malformation surgery will be required.

Eye Problems

All cats have the potential to suffer from eye problems. The most common include conjunctivitis, retinal infections, bacterial and viral infections. Glaucoma and cataracts are age related eye problems that need to be taken care of as early as possible to preserve your cat's eye sight for as long as possible. Common symptoms of an eye problem are:

- Cloudiness in the eye or eyes
- Redness of the eyelid linings
- Deposits in the corners of the eye
- Eyes that are watery
- Pawing at or rubbing the eye indicating pain or itching
- Squinting
- Keeping the eye closed or the inability to open it.

Standard preliminary treatment includes flushing the eye with water or a very mild saline solution and wiping away any deposits in the corner of the eye. If the problem continues, it is time to consult your vet.

Cats might also suffer injuries such as scratches to the eye if they are outdoors or have been in a fight. While very small scratches will heal on their own, marked or more serious eye injuries must be treated immediately!

Skin Problems

It's not always easy to spot a skin problem on a Chausie because of the very dense coat. However, signs to watch for are excessive scratching, flakes of dry skin in the fur, marked hair loss or even bald patches.

If your kitten or cat develops a rash of small red dots or lumps on the skin it might be that he or she has had an allergic reaction to something. Your Chausie could be having a reaction to a wide range of things but the usual culprits are:

o Bacteria: your vet can identify the type involved and treat the infection easily
o Flea bites: there are many products for this problem
o Ear mites: these can be found on the body too, especially in kittens. A definitive diagnosis should be done by a vet
o Food or diet: like people, some cats are allergic to certain foods or ingredients
o Shampoo: you could try hypoallergenic products designed for human babies
o New medication: if this is the case your vet may be able to use an alternative treatment
o Water or food bowls: some cats react badly to plastic. You could use stainless steel, glass or ceramic containers instead
o Household cleaning products: if a cat comes into contact with one of these it will irritate and inflame the skin. If the reaction is severe, take your cat to the vet. Alternatively wash the affected area gently and use a soothing lotion
o New or different cat litter: cats quite often react badly to litters that are either perfumed or contain a lot of dust that is stirred up when the cat digs in the litter

o Burns and heat rash: these can be caused by sources of heat, chemicals or overexposure to sun. If the burn is severe, take your cat to the vet immediately for pain relief and to prevent infection.

You can't protect your Chausie from all potential allergens. Also, you won't know what he or she is allergic to until they come into contact. All a loving cat owner can do is take precautions to prevent or at least limit exposure to possible allergens and then take the right steps if a cat does have a bad reaction to something.

7) More serious conditions

Inflammatory Bowl Disease (IBD)

The Chausie, especially F1 and F2 cats, may have shorter than standard intestinal tracts as the Jungle Cat and other wild cats so. This type of intestinal structure is thought to reduce the cat's ability to process ingredients that are derived from plants. So, vegetables, cereal, herbs and spices are not processed well or at all. These foodstuffs may trigger chronic intestinal inflammation and this in turn can lead to chronic inflammatory bowel disease.

Signs and symptoms

The signs and symptoms of IBD will vary depending on which part or parts of the digestive system are affected. For example, if the stomach is affected one of the primary symptoms will most likely be vomiting and if the colon is inflamed there will be in all probability be diarrhea. There may be mucous and / or blood in the stool.

Both of these symptoms may persist or come and go. A symptom that is usually found in cats suffering from IBD regardless of what organs are affected is weight loss. In severe and chronic cases cats will become lethargic, depressed, suffer from anemia, a fever, and, eventually, malnutrition as food is not absorbed by their systems.

Diagnosis

What makes diagnosis more difficult is that there are several types of IBD depending on the cause of the inflammation and where the inflammation is. In order to make a diagnosis several things are required:

- A full medical history to determine how long the problem has been going on and what the symptoms are.

- A thorough physical examination to assess body mass, any obvious thickening of the intestines, etc.

- Blood tests to see if the liver has been affected and to assess the protein levels and the electrolyte levels.

- X-rays do not usually assist in diagnosing this condition. However, ultrasound may show thickening or swelling in digestive organs and the presence of larger quantities of gas than are normal.

- The best single diagnostic tool for this condition is a biopsy which will show an increase in the number of inflammatory cells in the walls of the affected organ. Also, if an endoscope is used the vet will also see lesions on the lining of the organ.

Treatment

This illness can't be cured but it can be managed or controlled. There are two forms of management that are used with cats with IBD in order to ease the symptoms and prevent complications:

- o Diet: A vet may opt to try out various changes in diet to see which one the feline patient reacts best too. With the Chausie specifically it is usually a diet that is high in meat and contains no, or virtually no, cereals and vegetables. This may mean that all food is prepared by the cat's owner or a premium cat food may be used.

65

o Medication: The primary type of medication for IBD is corticosteroids (cortisone, steroids, for instance). They reduce the inflammation. Interestingly, cats don't usually suffer severe side effects to the drugs as dogs or people do! In addition, an antibiotic such as Metronidazole may be used to restore the natural bacterial balance in the intestine. Some symptoms are eased by the use of medication that treats diarrhea, vomiting and / or high levels of acidity.

Once the right diet has been found, the cat must stay on it as long as it continues to provide benefits. With any of the medications you should not stop giving them to your unless your vet says that it is alright to do so!

Polycystic Kidney Disease (PKD)

Polycystic Kidney Disease (PKD) is a serious genetic or inherited disease. It is a slowly progressive, irreversible disease.

Signs and symptoms

The signs of the disease do not usually appear until the cat is between the ages of 3 and 10 years even though it will have been born with abnormal kidneys. However, kittens that have very severely affected kidneys may die before they are 2 months old. Kidneys in kittens and cats that are affected by this illness contain numerous very small cysts that contain a clear or pale yellow fluid. Some may be filled with blood or become infected.

The cysts eventually take over from normal, healthy kidney tissue and the kidneys do not work properly. Eventually they fail entirely.

The signs of kidney failure are numerous and they include frequent urination, drinking more, not wanting to eat, lethargy, depression, weight loss and poor coat quality. There can also be vomiting and / or diarrhoea, seizures, blindness, anaemia, weakness and high blood pressure.

Diagnosis

Kidney failure is diagnosed using blood and urine tests. Polycystic Kidney Disease specifically is diagnosed from these tests and an ultrasound which will show the cysts. A medical examination is also performed which may show that the kidneys are irregular in shape or enlarged. An ultrasound can be performed on kittens as young as 6 weeks and will be 98% accurate in terms of diagnosis.

Treatment

The kidney cysts themselves can't be treated because they are so small and there are so many of them. However, kidney failure or some of the symptoms can be treated. Fluids are given to these cats intravenously to deal with any dehydration and electrolyte imbalances. Potassium, iron (to assist with anaemia) and calcium supplements are used when necessary. In addition, medications are used to control the vomiting and lower blood pressure.

Calcitriol is a medication that can be administered as it slows the progression of kidney failure. Finally, a diet of wet rather than dry food that is low in phosphorous and sodium, higher in dietary fatty acids and that contains very high quality protein is usually recommended.

The only way to prevent this horrible disease is for breeders to screen cats for the illness. Only cats that test negative for the gene that causes PKD should be used for breeding. Any cat found to have cysts or to be carrying the gene should be spayed or neutered to prevent the birth of kittens with either the disease or the gene.

Struvite Stones

Struvite stones are a form of bladder stone that are also called triple phosphate and magnesium phosphate stones. While they occur in both males and females, they are more common in female cats over the age of 6 years.

Signs and symptoms

Phosphate, ammonia and magnesium are all found in feline urine. However, in very high quantities they clump together and then form crystals. These cause irritation and inflammation in the bladder and can even form a plug that results in a potentially lethal blockage. When crystals bind together the result is a stone.

Causes

A common cause of struvite crystals or stones is a poor or inappropriate diet. However, these crystals or stones can also be the result of treatment with steroids, urine retention or a urinary tract infection or disorder of some kind. The symptoms are the same as for a urinary tract infection (see section 6 of this chapter).

Diagnosis

Diagnosis of struvite stones involves a careful examination to check for any enlargement of the bladder. In severe cases a vet can actually feel the stones when he probes the cat's abdomen with his fingers. In addition, a urine sample is tested to assess urine concentration levels and to look for blood, white blood cells, glucose, ketones, protein or bilirubin in the urine. All of these symptoms point to a diagnosis of these stones.

A urine culture is done if the blood test indicates an infection so that the specific bacteria involved can be treated. In the case of stones, ultrasound and x-rays will also be used to determine where the stones are in the urinary system and how large and what shape they are.

Treatment

Treatment depends on the findings of the vet and tests. If there is a blockage, immediate and emergency treatment is required. If the crystals or stones can be passed by the cat the usual course of action is medication and adjustments to the cat's diet. Some vets use homeopathy or natural remedies such as glucosamine or even cranberry extract. These help to lesson the inflammation in the bladder.

Changes to a cat's diet include ensuring the food does not contain grains or carbohydrates, reducing the amount of dry food because it increases urine concentration and giving the cat a moisture-rich diet.

These therapies are very effective in most cases but it can take several weeks, even months, before all the crystals or stones have broken down and been eliminated from the body. It is essential to continue to give the cat the medication and maintain the diet until your cat's vet confirms that recovery is complete. It is then important to guard against any reoccurrences of the problem.

Stones that have lodged in the urethra or ureters, which are the tubes that connect the kidneys to the bladder, often have to be removed surgically or with laser treatment. This is also necessary in cases where diet changes and medication have not dissolved or dealt with the stones. The most invasive surgical procedure to remove a stone is called cystotomy. Lasers can break down smaller stones which can then pass with relative ease. The final option is a procedure that involves manually squeezing the stones out. This is called voiding urohydropropulsion. All three options are carried out under anaesthetic.

Hip Dysplasia

With this condition the hip joints do not develop normally and the ball and socket of the joint actually become dislocated. Due to this malformation the joints gradually deteriorate and eventually do not function at all.

Causes

While environmental factors such as diet and obesity can play a role, this condition – like Polycystic Kidney Disease – is usually due to genetic factors. In this case, however, more than one gene is involved and a kitten will inherit the gene from both parents even if neither has hip dysplasia. The condition is more common in purebreds, in females and in breeds that have heavy bones or bodies like the Chausie.

Signs and symptoms

Symptoms vary and are affected by the degree of inflammation, how long the cat has had the condition and, finally, how loose the hip joint has become. Common symptoms include:

- Pain
- Decreased levels of activity
- Difficulty standing up
- Reluctance to jump, run or climb stairs
- A hopping or swaying walk
- Stiffness and decreased movement in the hips
- A grating sound as the hip joint moves
- Loss of muscle in the back legs and an increase in muscle in the front legs and shoulders
- Lameness.

Diagnosis

This condition is diagnosed through blood tests including a full blood count and blood chemical profile, a urine test and a complete physical examination. The vet will also get a full medical history from you in terms of when the problem started and the symptoms you have seen. The blood count will give evidence of the inflammation caused by the affected joint. X-rays will confirm hip dysplasia and show the degree of abnormality or dislocation.

Treatment

Treatment is usually on an outpatient basis unless surgery is necessary. Various factors will determine whether or not surgery is an option. These include the cat's age and size, how severe the dysplasia and osteoarthritis are and – sometimes – the financial considerations of the owner. Physiotherapy is an alternative for some cats as it can help to improve muscle tone and reduce stiffness in the joint. Vets often also prescribe medication for both pain and inflammation.

Cats suffering from this condition must not be allowed to become overweight as this places additional strain on the hip joints. A vet must work with the cat owner on diet as the cat will be less active and therefore more prone to gain weight.

Regardless of whether a cat has had surgery or more conservative treatment, a vet needs to monitor the cat's condition. X-rays are taken regularly for comparison purposes to see if the condition is worsening.

Because this condition has a genetic cause, cats that suffer from it should not be used for breeding and should be sterilized.

Medial Patellar Luxation (MPL)

Medial patella luxation (MPL) is the dislocation of the patella or knee cap in the back legs. Normally the knee cap moves in a groove in the femur (the large bone in the lower leg that goes ends at the knee joint). With MPL the knee cap is displaced and moves sideways, usually to the inside of the knee joint. This displacement can be partial or complete and might be an intermittent or a permanent problem.

Causes

With the Chausie this condition is genetic and develops fairly early in the cat's life. It can also be caused by an injury like being hit by a car. The symptoms range in severity from a skip-like limp to complete lameness. With congenital MPL more than one knee is affected.

Diagnosis

Diagnosis is made through a careful examination, including watching the cat walk and run and comparing the knees when the cat is standing. The vet will also gently manipulate the affected leg or legs in order to test the range of motion in the joint as this gives an idea of severity. X-rays will also be done to assess the degree of luxation or displacement.

Treatment

A cat that has mild MPL will be rested and treated with anti-inflammatories. However, surgery is necessary with severe MPL that has caused lameness and where there is the start of arthritis in the affected knee(s). The nature and extent of the surgery depends on the individual case and could involve deepening the groove in the femur, the tendon that attaches to the knee cap might be cut and reattached or joint capsule may be altered.

After surgery your Chausie will need nursing at home. The dressing on the wound must be kept clean and dry to avoid any infection. If you notice the toes on the affected leg or legs are swelling or sore you need to contact your vet. You need to check for this twice a day. Finally, leave your cat to rest and don't play games as exercise must be restricted for up to 6 weeks after surgery.

In the case of genetic or hereditary MPL an affected cat should not be used for breeding as the condition may be passed on to the offspring.

Feline Infectious Peritonitis (FIP)

Causes

FIP is caused by infection of a cat by the Feline Coronavirus virus, which is very common in cats.

Signs and symptoms

Often the only symptom will be mild diarrhoea. However, in rare cases the virus mutates and causes Feline Infectious Peritonitis. 80% of cats who contract FIP are younger than 2 years old.

Once a cat is infected, the virus spreads throughout the body and causes a range of symptoms including peritonitis, which is an accumulation of fluid in the abdomen. In some cases the fluid gathers in the chest cavity not the abdomen. In other cats the brain, eyes, liver, kidneys or other organs become inflamed.

Ordinarily, this virus mainly infects the intestinal tract, where it thrives and then replicates or multiplies. The virus is shed in the faeces and may survive in the outside environment for several days or even a few weeks. However, it is destroyed by common disinfectants. Infection is caused when a cat ingests the virus when grooming. Some cats will always be infected but they become immune to the virus. Other cats will become infected, recover and then be re-infected. In the majority of cases there will be no symptoms other than mild diarrhoea.

FIP is a very serious complication of a Feline Coronavirus infection. In this situation the virus no longer stays in the digestive tract; it mutates and spreads throughout the body. What is difficult is that none of the symptoms a cat will exhibit are unique to FIP. Early signs, for example, include lack of appetite, lethargy and a fluctuating fever. It can take anywhere from a few days to several months before other symptoms appear.

There are two forms of FIP: 'wet' or 'effusive' disease and 'dry' or 'non-effusive' disease. Cats often have a mix of these two types. With 'wet' FIP fluid collects in the abdominal or chest cavity. This results in distension and breathing difficulty respectively. The liquid that collects is due to damaged and inflamed blood vessels that leak fluid. 'Dry' FIP usually causes chronic lesions around blood vessels in various parts of the body, which lead to a type of inflammation. This inflammation can affect the eyes; the brain; tissues in the liver, kidneys, lungs and skin and even neurological disease.

Diagnosis

Because symptoms are not unique to the disease, diagnosis is done on the basis of these symptoms and a battery of blood tests that look at white blood cell counts, protein levels in the blood, signs of jaundice or liver problems and liver enzyme levels. Often some of the fluid collecting in the abdomen or chest is analysed too.

A vet may also take X-rays or an ultrasound to assess fluid collection. Only if a combination of all these symptoms and results are found can a diagnosis be made. Another diagnostic option is a biopsy of affected tissue to examine it for the Feline Coronavirus virus itself. However, a cat is usually too sick for a procedure as invasive as this.

Treatment

The disease is rapid and progressive. There is no cure for FIP and not much that can be done to ease the cat's suffering other than the use of anti-inflammatory drugs. Usually euthanasia is the most humane course of action to avoid suffering.

There is a vaccine that is available in some countries to help protect against FIP that can be given to kittens over 16 weeks of age. This vaccination is especially important in breeding households or where there are large groups of cats.

Feline Leukaemia Virus (FeLV)

Amongst cats in general, Feline leukaemia virus is the second leading cause of death in cats with the lead cause being trauma.

Causes

Transmission is through saliva, blood, urine and faeces to a lesser degree. It is therefore most often spread during grooming or if an infected cat gets into a fight. It is not transmitted to people or dogs. Kittens can contract the virus before birth from an infected mother or after birth from her milk. Older cats are less likely to be infected; for some reason resistance increases with age. Indoor cats are far less likely to contract the virus.

Signs and symptoms

This virus commonly causes anaemia (low red blood cells) or lymphoma (a group of blood cell tumours). It also suppresses the immune system which leaves cats open to a host of infections. The good news is that about 70% of cats who contract Feline leukaemia survive.

The symptoms of Feline leukaemia include appetite and weight loss, diarrhoea, pale gums or yellowish colour in the mouth and eyes, fever, breathing problems, swollen glands, infections (skin, bladder or upper respiratory tract) and unsprayed females can become sterile.

Diagnosis

This disease is diagnosed through a blood test, called ELISA, which is done by a vet. The test looks for FeLV proteins in the blood and is able to pick infection up in the early stages. The IFA blood test is used to detect the illness if it is at the advanced stage. If the result of this test is positive for the virus the outlook or prognosis for the infected cat is not good.

Treatment

Unfortunately, 85% of the cats that suffer from a persistent FeLV infection will not survive for longer than 3 years. But, regular vet visits, care and good nutrition to provide them with a good quality of life and guard against any secondary infections. These cats, though, must be kept indoors and spayed or neutered if they have not already been sterilised. As you will have gathered, there is no cure for FeLV. Treatment is supportive and used to improve quality of life and fight secondary infections.

Feline Immunodeficiency Virus (FIV)

This virus is a complex retrovirus that leads to immunodeficiency disease in cats. In other words, cats infected with this virus cat develop or maintain a normal immune response to protect themselves from infections.

Causes

A cat can become infected through bites and scratches from an infected cat, in utero or when suckling from an infected mother, and – far less commonly – during sexual contact as the virus has been detected in semen.

Signs and symptoms

The symptoms of FIV are diverse and can be confused with those for other illnesses. For instance, some of the infections these cats pick up are similar to those suffered by cats with Feline leukaemia virus. Recurring minor gastrointestinal and upper respiratory tract problems are common as are swollen or enlarged lymph nodes or glands. There can also be inflammation of the gums, especially the area of tissue around the teeth.

In more advanced cases there is upper respiratory tract disease and marked inflammation of various tissues including the eye, cornea, nose, glaucoma (increased pressure within the eyeball), persistent diarrhoea, chronic kidney problems and fungal infections affecting the cat's skin and / or ears.

There is also usually fever and, as the disease progresses, marked weight loss. Certain types of cancers can develop, particularly in the lymphatic system, and changes to the nervous system can cause disrupted sleep and behaviour patterns, increased aggression, loss of hearing and disorders affecting the nerves in the legs and feet.

Diagnosis

Diagnosis of FIV is achieved by taking a detailed medical history, doing a thorough examination, blood tests including a blood profile and count and analysing the cat's urine. Before a final diagnosis is made, a vet must rule our parasites, tumours and infections caused by bacteria, fungi or other viruses.

Treatment

Treatment of a cat with Feline immunodeficiency virus takes place on an outpatient basis unless the cat is dangerously dehydrated. The first job for the vet is to deal with secondary infections before they become serious or cause complications. If necessary, surgery is done to remove tumours and badly infected teeth. Cats living with this illness will also be placed on a specifically formulated diet.

As an owner of a cat with FIV one needs to watch one's cat for recurring or additional secondary infections or any other symptoms. An infected cat must also be kept on its special diet and seen regularly by a vet so that its condition is monitored. If the diagnosis is made fairly early, cats with this illness can live long and relatively healthy lives.

The main focus of prevention is a vaccination. In addition to this keeping your cat indoors and away from cats that are or may be infected is the second line of defence.

Hyperthyroidism

Hyperthyroidism or an overactive thyroid gland is a common disorder, particularly in cats over the age of seven, and affects both males and females.

Causes

The thyroid glands in the neck increase their production of the hormones that regulate many of the body's processes. When there is too much of the hormone the effects and symptoms can be severe. Some cats become seriously ill, but fortunately most cats that that develop this condition can be treated and recover fully.

The cause of the condition in over 70% of cats is a benign or non-cancerous change in the thyroid glands. At this stage it is not clear what brings this change about. Unlike humans who only have one thyroid gland, cats have two of these glands. With this change in the older cat's body the glands become enlarged in addition to producing too much hormone. In a very small number of cats (1 to 2%) the disease is caused by a cancerous tumour in one or both of the glands.

Signs and symptoms

Symptoms appear gradually and, if the condition is not treated, worsen over time. One of the body systems or processes the thyroid controls is metabolic rate. Cats suffering from this problem burn energy too fast and therefore get very thin despite being hungry and eating a lot. In addition to constant hunger and weight loss, other symptoms are a marked increase in thirst levels, greater activity that can appear more like restlessness, irritability, increased heart rate and the coat looks uncared for and there may be hair loss. In more severe cases cats become very heat sensitive or intolerant, will develop diarrhoea and vomiting and may even pant. There can also be weakness and lethargy.

If hyperthyroidism is left untreated it is potentially lethal for a cat as there can be complications. Cats can develop hypertension or high blood pressure. Untreated raised blood pressure can damage the kidneys, eyes, brain and the heart itself. The increased heart rate causes changes in the muscles of the heart wall. Eventually this can lead to heart failure. Medication is needed to control the blood pressure.

Diagnosis

Although this condition usually results in enlarged glands they are rarely visible. A vet will be able to detect it when he or she does a careful examination. However, a check up is not always enough so blood tests are also used. The primary test measures the level of thyroid hormones (thyroxin or T4) in the blood.

A further blood test that is sometimes required examines liver enzymes and liver health. A vet will also often perform a urine test to check kidney function, measure blood pressure and – in severe cases – a chest x-ray or an ultrasound.

Treatment

The good news is that with treatment all the signs and symptoms disappear. Periodic blood tests are performed, though, as the condition does not go away. The vet will monitor thyroxin levels and kidney function on an ongoing basis. There are currently four main treatment options:

➤ *Medication*: The most commonly used and effective anti-thyroid drugs are in the group called thioamides which includes both methimazole and carbimazole. Both are widely used in the management of feline hyperthyroidism. These drugs reduce the production and release of thyroid hormones and so control the illness. They are not a cure but they are effective and safe.

   To control the disease the medication must be given daily and often twice daily. While side effects are uncommon they can include decreased appetite, lethargy and vomiting. The side effects stop after the first few weeks of treatment. More serious side effects are extremely rare.

➤ *Surgical thyroidectomy*: The surgical removal of the affected parts of the thyroid glands can result in a cure. As a result it is a common treatment for many hyperthyroid cats. However, occasionally signs of hyperthyroidism develop again at a later stage because thyroid tissue that was not diseased before is affected.

   To reduce anaesthetic and surgical complications, cats are ideally stabilised with anti-thyroid drug therapy before surgery is carried out. If the cat is suffering from heart disease this must also be addressed before the procedure. The major risk associated with the surgery itself is accidentally damaging the parathyroid glands, which are small glands close to or even inside the thyroid glands. The parathyroid glands are essential to maintain stable blood calcium levels.

Because there is a small risk of temporary interference with calcium regulation postoperatively, cats usual remain hospitalised for a few days after surgery. The cat's overall health and recovery and monitored in addition to the blood calcium concentrations. Occasional blood tests are recommended by vets in order to ensure that normal thyroid hormone levels are being maintained.

➤ *Radioactive iodine therapy*: Radioactive iodine (I-131) sounds scary but it is a very safe and effective treatment for hyperthyroidism. The first benefit is that it is usually a once-off treatment and – in most cases – a permanent cure. In fact, a single injection cures in the region of 95% of all cats suffering from hyperthyroidism.

The radioactive iodine is administered as an injection that is given under the skin. The iodine is only absorbed by the abnormal thyroid tissue. The radiation then destroys the affected thyroid tissue but it does not damage any of the surrounding tissues or the parathyroid glands.

There are no significant side-effects with this treatment, but because the cat is temporarily radioactive it must, as a precaution, be kept at the clinic or vet for a short time after treatment. It is recommended that occasional blood tests are done after treatment to make sure normal thyroid hormone levels are being maintained

➤ *Dietary treatment*: A new and more recent option for the management of hyperthyroid cats is to feed them on a special diet with strictly controlled levels of iodine. The logic behind this is that iodine is used by the thyroid gland to make thyroid hormones. If there is only enough iodine in the cat's diet to make normal levels of thyroxin the disease can be controlled.

This is a new and so far promising new treatment. It does mean that the owner must exclusively feed the cat a special therapeutic diet that is only available from a vet.

If a cat's hyperthyroidism is caused by a malignant, cancerous tumour (a thyroid adenocarcinoma) then treatment is far more difficult and success is less certain. Treatments involving very high doses of radioactive iodine have shown good results.

Feline diabetes mellitus

There are two types of diabetes mellitus in cats and they are not the same as the types of diabetes found in people.

Causes, signs and symptoms

The first is Type I or Insulin-dependent Diabetes Mellitus (IDDM). This is the form of diabetes that affects 50 to 75% of diabetic cats. The cause of IDDM is the loss of beta cells in the pancreas. These cells produce insulin and without them a cat must have insulin treatment or it will die. Cats with this type of diabetes are often very thin and they can develop serious conditions (ketoacidosis) because of the body's inability to use fat instead of glucose for energy.

Type II is Non-insulin-dependent Diabetes Mellitus (NIDDM). This affects the remaining 50 to 25% of cats with diabetes. Unlike with IDDM, these cats still have beta cells in the pancreas but the insulin response to a high blood sugar or glucose level is not normal. With this type there is a delay in insulin secretion when the blood glucose starts to increase, followed by excess insulin secretion. The cells of the body also do not react normally to insulin.

Cats with NIDDM survive without additional insulin but therapy is often used to ease the symptoms and maintain weight control.

Some cats with NIDDM can be successfully treated with diet changes. Cats with type II diabetes are usually overweight and rarely need insulin to survive. The danger with this type is that the beta cells may die and the cat could progress to IDDM.

Some cats develop Secondary Diabetes Mellitus. This happens when another illness results in the destruction of or damage to beta cells in the pancreas. Some of the illnesses that can cause secondary diabetes are hyperthyroidism, Cushing's disease, pancreatitis or acromegaly (a production of too much growth hormone). The cat may or may not need insulin treatment depending on how serious the damage to the pancreas is. In addition, secondary diabetes is reversible in some cases.

There are various signs and symptoms of diabetes mellitus in cats:

➤ *Increased thirst and urination*: glucose can't enter the cells so levels in the blood become far too high. The kidneys then filter out the glucose. Because the cat urinates more it needs to drink more.

➤ *Inappropriate elimination*: the fact that the cat is urinating more often means that there may be accidents in the house. Diabetic cats are also prone to urinary tract infections which can also lead to urination outside a litter box.

➤ *Appetite changes*: some diabetic cats eat less because they don't feel well. Other cats suddenly eat far more than before.

➤ *Weight loss*: due to the illness the cat can't use the calories consumed for energy. Instead body fat is broken down and used as fuel for the body. As fat is used the cat becomes thinner.

➤ *Change in gait*: the disease can result in nervous system abnormalities which makes the cat walk with their hocks almost touching the ground. Vets call the condition causing this strange almost crouching gait diabetic neuropathy.

> *Weakness, lethargy and depression*: the cat feels weak and without energy because he or she is unable to use the food it eats. Some diabetic cats also loose muscle and this contributes to weakness. If the cat is also depressed it may well stop grooming and no longer be interested in things around it.

> *Vomiting*: cats with severe diabetes that are breaking down the fat in their own bodies for energy have waste products – called ketones – that begin to accumulate as a result. Ketones in the blood cause nausea and vomiting. If the level of ketones in the blood gets very high and the pH drops. This increase in acidity leads to a life-threatening condition called ketoacidosis.

Common symptoms of ketoacidosis are loss of appetite, vomiting, diarrhoea, weakness, change in respiration, dehydration, and sometimes collapse. In severe cases, you will be able to smell of acetone on the cat's breath. A cat suffering ketoacidosis is an emergency case and no time should be lost. These cats require around the clock care and monitoring. Treatment will involve insulin, intravenous fluids, medications that reduce potassium levels to normal and sometimes antibiotics are also needed because these cats are very prone to infections.

Diagnosis

Diagnosis of feline diabetes mellitus is based on the presence of persistently high blood glucose levels (hyperglycaemia) even when the cat has not eaten recently, glucose in the urine (glycosuria) and common signs and symptoms. Symptoms alone are not enough because they are similar to those found with kidney failure and hyperthyroidism. Diagnosis consists of several aspects:

> A full medical history
> A thorough physical examination
> Blood and urine tests.

The blood and urine tests are usually done more than once as the glucose levels need to be persistently high for a diagnosis to be made. The tests also look at liver enzymes, raised cholesterol, and whether the levels of sodium, potassium and phosphorous are lower than normal.

A classification of insulin-dependent, non-insulin dependent or secondary diabetes cannot be clearly made for some cats. This is because there is a spectrum of disease that ranges from severely insulin dependent, to requiring small doses of insulin, to requiring none.

In addition, the insulin-dependence of a cat might change over the course of its life as it moves slowly from, for example, non-insulin-dependent diabetes to insulin-dependent diabetes. There are also some cases of transient diabetes where a cat needs insulin for a while and then, after a few months or even a year, they no longer need this treatment.

8) Obesity in Chausie cats

The effect of being overweight or obese on the health and general well-being of any cat is always negative. Besides the usual problems like sluggishness and lethargy, obesity in cats has several associated health disorders. Fortunately Chausies are very active and playful cats and this should go a long way to ensuring that he or she gets the necessary amount of exercise.

Sometimes it becomes very difficult to determine if your cat is overweight, especially through all that gorgeous thick fur. Obesity is harder to miss! Just because the cat's levels of activity and agility seem to be fine doesn't mean that it is not chubbier than it should be.

There are reliable ways of telling if your cat is becoming obese. You can try three simple tests at home before you have an actual expert test your cat for obesity. It's important to monitor your cat's weight on an ongoing basis as you might miss a gradual weight gain.

How to tell if your Chausie is overweight

Step number one is to feel the area around the rib cage of your cat. If you are still able to feel the rib cage through his or her fur, it means that he or she is not obese. However, if you have to press really hard to get to the rib cage, it means that your cat is heavier than the normal, acceptable weight.

Secondly, a cat's waistline should have a distinct shape: the body tapers from the belly towards the hind quarters. If a cat is too tubby and the body extends evenly from belly to the rear quarters and pelvis, it is a sign that your cat needs to lose weight.

A hanging pouch between the hind legs of a cat is a definite sign the cat is overweight. If the pouch is more like a flap of skin rather than a fat-filled pouch it probably means that your older cat was too fat, lost the weight but the skin had stretched.

Like humans, cats that are overweight will experience several health issues. Therefore, you must take the necessary measures to slim your cat down and maintain a healthy weight.

Obesity related health problems

One of the most common complaints in veterinary clinics across the globe is health disorders related to obesity. The biggest threat to the wellbeing of cats is feline diabetes mellitus. The second most prevalent disorder in cats due to obesity is hyperthyroidism which is due to excessive production of thyroid.

According to experts, the chances of an obese cat becoming diabetic are double in comparison to cats that have a normal weight. This risk becomes 8 times higher if the cat becomes severely obese. The association between obesity and diabetes is quite evident. When your cat becomes obese, there is a drastic increase in the amount of inflammatory markers and oxidative stress. This causes insulin resistance which leads to obesity.

The resistance to insulin is one of the most common problems found in cats. It has also been observed that a change in diet is not as effective in increasing insulin sensitivity as the actual reduction in weight.

There are several other health conditions that can be found in cats due to feline obesity:

Osteoarthritis and lameness: This condition occurs because there is too much stress on the medium sized frame of your Chausie. You will be able to hear loud thuds when your cat jumps off a table or chair which indicates a gradual loss of agility in the cat.

Liver and urinary system: Too much pressure on the liver also causes liver problems like feline lipidosis syndrome. Also, urinary tract disorders are common in cats that are obese.

The biggest issue with obesity is not the condition itself. The inability of many owners to recognize this condition and provide necessary treatment is the cause for the drastic increase in feline obesity in the last couple of years. There are many cases that have been reported where owners are just used to over-feeding their cat. They actually think that normal sized cats look malnourished and unhealthy. As the owner, it is your responsibility to evaluate the condition of your cat's body on a regular basis. You can also get a body condition score to check for the amount of fat present in your cat's body. These scores show the difference in the calorie intake of your cat and the actual energy requirement. If your Chausie is being overfed, the score will go up to indicate an increase in fat deposits.

How to keep your Chausie at a healthy weight

It is actually not very difficult to maintain your cat's normal body weight. All you need to do is ensure that the width of the hips and shoulders are maintained without any visible bulge on the sides.

You must also make sure that the belly of your cat does not hang too low. The Chausie is a muscular but long and lean cat so fat deposits become clearly evident early on. Once you have spotted it there are fortunately a few things you can do to reduce obesity in your cat.

Firstly, you need to understand what the right amount of food for your cat is. The quantity of food that you give your cat should be just enough to keep it healthy. It is impossible to quantify the amount of food that one should give a Chausie as the cat's age, gender, state of health, activity levels etcetera all impact on this. However, you can measure the calorie intake in your cat if need be. Your vet or a local breeder or association can advise you as to how many kilocalories per kilo of body weight your cat should be getting.

Depending on your cat's health, you can determine how much food it requires. If there has been any recent surgical procedure or neutering / spaying, you must make sure you reduce the food intake accordingly.

Free choice feeding is a very common problem. Cat owners, out of love, provide their cat with a range of flavours and choices. This often leads to over eating. In addition, if you mix dry cat food with canned food there is a chance of overeating. Similarly, constant changes in the taste of foods will make your cat overeat because of the novelty. Like us, cats find it hard to resist a great tasting meal.

Using a measuring cup to judge portion size and so ensure that your cat is neither over fed nor under fed can be very helpful. However, if you prefer free choice feeding, divide the food into two portions. Give your cat one helping in the morning and one in the evening. You must also be very careful that the feeding is age appropriate. Depending on whether you have a kitten or a senior cat in your household, the choice of diet will vary.

The importance of keeping your cat hydrated can't be stressed enough. You must make sure that there is plenty of fresh water available for your cat, especially if you are feeding it dry cat food, While most dry foods work very well for cats, lack of water might lead to issues like urinary tract disorders and also lowered kidney function.

Water is an essential nutrient for your Chausie. Irrespective of whether you are feeding it wet or dry food, you must give it enough water. The presence of adequate amounts of water in the body will help your cat process and absorb the food that it has eaten. Proper digestion and elimination, which is the key to good health in a cat, is regulated by the amount of water available.

If you have put your cat on a weight loss diet, you must give him adequate amounts of protein. It is true that the calorie intake must be restricted. However, you must always make sure that you do not reduce the amount of essential nutrients. When you increase the amount of proteins, weight loss is aided while keeping the lean body mass intact.

If you are concerned about the weight and health of your Chausie, make sure you reduce the amount of treats and titbits. This practice must be extended to at least a couple of weeks after the 'diet' period. You must make sure that everyone in your family is aware of this rule.

If you try and cheat out of affection, remember that you are harming your cat's health. It would help, instead, to cut your cat's meals down to smaller, more frequent meals. This will ensure that it does not experience hunger pangs while continuing to stay on a healthy diet.

Crash diets are as harmful for cats and they are for humans. You must never starve your cat. In fact, no matter what restrictions you make in its diet, it must be supervised by a dietician. If you don't carefully monitor the amount of minerals and vitamins your cat is getting it can lead to a fatal condition called hepatic lipidosis, which affects the liver.

Exercise is extremely important in cats. You cannot control the health and weight of your Chausie by only altering its diet. You must also ensure that it has an active lifestyle. As indicated earlier, you will have your Chausie's full cooperation in this regard! So, you will be both controlling the calories your cat takes in and making sure that he or she burns the calories through exercise and activity.

One can do a number of things to encourage activity and to keep your cat's environment stimulating and engaging:

- To begin with, set aside a dedicated time to play with your cat or cats. You can use simple toys like strings to help your Chausie play and get a good workout. (You will probably get one too!)

- In addition, allow his or her natural instincts to take over; let your cat climb, jump, pounce, scratch and even chase around the house. These exercises are interesting and fun for your cat and will increase the process of weight loss.

- It is suggested that cat owners get a feeding ball to give a cat one meal in the day. The advantage with the feeding ball is that your cat will have to put in some effort to roll the ball and get to the food inside.

- Also, you could place your cat's food bowl at the top of a flight of stairs. This will encourage your Chausie to climb to get to the food.

Throughout the process of weight loss, you must be extremely patient. It will take several weeks and even months for your cat to lose weight.

If you find it too hard to maintain the weight of your cat on your own, you can ask your vet for tips. You could even enrol your Chausie in a veterinary weight loss clinic for additional support and information.

9) *How to give your Chausie medication*

Giving medication to a cat can be a challenge. One needs to try and do so in a way that will not stress or hurt your cat… or you!

In order to give your Chausie a pill or tablet, hold your cat against your body and on a surface that is about waist height to you. Place the thumb and fingers of one hand on either side of your cat's mouth. If you press gently with your fingers and tilt the cat's head back, its mouth should open automatically. Using your other hand, gently pull the lower jaw down and place the pill or tablet as far back on the tongue as you can.

Continue to hold the head back and keep your cat's mouth closed until you are sure that he or she has swallowed the medication. When you let go watch your cat for a minute or so in case he or she spits the pill out.

If you need to give a liquid medication, tip the cat's head back. Open his or her mouth as you would for a pill or tablet. Then gently pull out a corner of the lower lip to form a pocket. Pour the liquid medicine into the pocket in the lip and then hold your cat's mouth closed until he or she has swallowed. Don't try to administer so much at once that most of the dose is spilled before it has a chance to go into the mouth.

If you need to restrain a cat, for whatever reason, wrap it in a soft blanket with only the part of the cat you need to deal with exposed. Make sure that it is tight enough to prevent the cat escaping easily but not so tight that it causes pain or discomfort.

10) *How to clean your cat's teeth*

Like any other cat, the Chausie is susceptible to problems with its teeth and gums. The most common of these is gingivitis or gum inflammation.

This condition is caused by the build up of plaque mixed with saliva and food particles on the teeth. If this substance hardens into tartar and builds up along the gum line the gums become inflamed and even infected. This can cause pain and bleeding and your cat may find eating painful. If periodontal disease goes unchecked your cat will eventually lose his or her teeth.

The vet can remove tartar by using a procedure known as descaling. However, if you practice good dental hygiene from the time your Chausie is a kitten you can avoid any serious oral or dental diseases.

It is very important that you begin to clean your Chausie's teeth when he or she is still a baby. This way, at least your cat will be used to it even though it will never enjoy it. It is best to clean a cat's teeth daily. The absolute minimum is twice a week.

The best way to handle the dental routine is to collect all the supplies you will need in advance before you tackle your cat. Some cat owners use sterile gauze strips to clean their cat's teeth. Others begin with gauze and move, as their cat becomes more tolerant, to a soft rubber toothbrush. You can buy toothbrushes and toothpaste from your vet. Please note that you should never under any circumstances use toothpaste that is designed for people as this could be very dangerous, even fatal, for your cat!

In order to get a kitten used to the sensation of having something in its mouth, you can begin by just using your little finger which you have dipped into something the kitten will enjoy the taste of. For example, you could use the brine solution that tinned tuna comes in. Once your kitten has become used to this, begin to wrap gauze around your finger which also has been soaked in the solution the kitten will like. To begin with, only clean one or two teeth in a session and then gradually increase the number of teeth you work on.

In order to clean your kitten or cat's teeth, either wrap a strip of gauze around your index finger or use the toothbrush. Dip either the gauze or toothbrush into the feline toothpaste a saline solution. With the cat on your lap, gently open its jaw and rub your finger or the toothbrush on each tooth using a circular motion. You need to pay particular attention to the areas next to the gum where tartar builds up. You need to be thorough but gentle enough that you do not damage the gums.

As with all the hygiene and health care procedures you do with your cat you must remember to make comforting sounds and talk soothingly to him and her while you were working. Afterwards you need to praise him or her and make time for cuddles and even playing a game. Your cat should enjoy the rewards so much that he or she is willing to endure this hygiene routine in order to have the fun afterwards!

11) The self-medicating cat

We've all seen cats eating grass and many of us assume that it is something they do when their tummies aren't feeling quite right. All cats eat grass, but the experts are not entirely sure why.

Eating grass certainly seems to help cats that need to regurgitate hair they have swallowed. A considerable amount of grass consisting of whole blades does have an emetic effect. It is also possible that when they just nibble at the tips of grass cats are taking in the roughage that they feel they need in order to regulate their digestive systems. Another theory is that they get additional trace elements and vitamins from grass and they instinctively know when they need them.

Whatever the reason, it appears that cats need and want to eat grass on occasion. If you don't have a garden or your cat is purely an indoor cat you will need to plant a window box or a pot with suitable grass for your kitty to snack on.

12) De-clawing a cat

In a word: don't! The process of de-clawing a cat involves the surgical amputation of the first joint of every digit on the cat's front feet. In other words, it is a mutilation of the cat that causes considerable post-operative pain and possible phantom pain the rest of its life. If you train your cat properly and supply it with a scratching post there is absolutely no acceptable reason to have this procedure done.

This practice is followed in order to prevent the cat from damaging furniture and property. Other pet owners also justify declawing a cat as a method of protecting other people from being scratched or hurt by their cat. In some residential properties, people are not allowed to keep cats unless they are completely declawed.

It is quite certain that those who advocate declawing do not understand the seriousness of this procedure. It is not a way of keeping the nails trimmed or blunt. It is a medical surgery that has horrible repercussions for the cat. It is permanent and irreversible. There is also no guarantee that your Chausie will ever recover entirely from this traumatic experience. For this reason, several European countries have strong laws against declawing the cat.

If you have considered declawing or had it suggested to you, remember that the toes and claws are an important part of the anatomy of the cat that makes it more agile and graceful. The claws allow cats to get purchase on surfaces. Declawing also deprives a cat of its instinctive defence mechanism: the ability to climb a tree to escape danger at ground level and to also to use its claws to scratch an attacker and defend itself.

The recuperation period following de-clawing is very hard and painful. The short-, medium- and long-term impact on the cat is significant.

For up to three days after the surgery, the cat will suffer post procedure lameness and will drag itself around. A cat will not lose its instinctive behaviour even if it is in pain. It will therefore still need to walk, jump and scratch despite the pain. It will also have to use the litter box. This will impact on recovery time.

Almost 80% of cats that have undergone declawing have developed complications after surgery or even after discharge that were caused by the wrong sheering techniques being used or even the nature of the blade used for surgery. The most common conditions include abscesses, necrosis (death) of tissue, growth of deformed claws, motor paralysis, nerve damage, haemorrhage, stress induced bladder inflammation, infections, swelling and even reluctance to walk.

Furthermore, there have been reports that declawing can change the cat's personality including that of cats that were previously loving and gentle:

> ➢ The biting frequency and strength increases in most cats. The only possible explanation to this is that when a cat loses one form of defence, it activates another.

> ➢ House soiling is twice as common in declawed cats. Firstly, they become reluctant to walk and put pressure on their paws. In addition to that, severe cases like nerve dysfunction and even lameness leave the cat helpless.

> ➢ Aggression is very common in cats post declawing. The pain makes them more defensive against people. Also, the fact that you, their owner and the person who should take care of and protect them, inflicted that pain on him or her makes you less trustworthy in the eyes of your cat and the cat generally less trusting and far more anxious.

Almost 45% of cats in America that have been declawed are referred to vet teaching hospitals and cat schools to sort out behavioural issues. The change in behaviour is more drastic if the cat has undergone tendonectomy in the process of being declawed. The repercussions of these behaviour changes include relinquishing cats to shelters. For a cat like the Chausie, which gets particularly attached to people, this experience is extremely traumatic.

There are alternatives to declawing a cat.

✓ Trim your cat's nails with a nail clipper. This will reduce the damage caused by your cat's claws to a large extent.

✓ Another simple option is to provide your cat with a scratching post. You can attract your cat to the scratching post by using scent sprays that smell like catnip. A sisal scratch post is most recommended for cats as the roughness of the surface is just right for the cat to fulfil its urge to scratch something.

✓ One of the simplest and most effective solutions are nail caps made of vinyl that you can simply glue to the front claws of your cat. It is best recommended for those who have cats like the Chausie that spend a lot of their time indoors. You can even protect your children from the cat with the help of "Soft Claws" or a similar product available from a vet or good pet shop. Once these caps wear off, they can be simply replaced with a new set.

✓ Train your cat. That is the best way to protect your space and others from the claws of the cat. Teach your cat to only use the scratch post. You can also train it to be at its best behaviour when it is around strangers.

For a cat like the Chausie all of these alternatives work well. In case your cat is in the habit of venturing outside, you might want to avoid clipping the nails or even using nail caps so that your cat can be on guard.

13) A first aid kit for your cat

First aid items for your cat should be stored in a suitable container that is easily accessible, portable and clearly marked. It is also recommended that a feline first aid kit should include the following items although others can of course be added if you find them useful:

o Antibiotic powder
o Antiseptic wash
o Cat laxative
o Eye dropper

o   Gauze swabs
o   Hydrogen peroxide 3%
o   Mercurochrome
o   Roll of cotton wool or absorbent cotton
o   Roll of adhesive bandage (2.5 cm or 1" wide)
o   Roll of adhesive bandage (7.5 cm or 3" wide)
o   Roll of gauze bandage (2.5 cm or 1" wide)
o   Sharp, pointed scissors
o   Round tip scissors
o   20 ml plastic syringe
o   Thermometer
o   Anti-bacterial and anti-fungal solution such as tincture of iodine
o   Torch or flashlight
o   Tweezers.

In order to maintain the kit, you will need to clean any instrument that you have used before putting it back in the kit. If any of the consumables are used, replace them the same day.

It is also advisable to check the kit contents every six months to ensure that everything is in order, nothing has expired and that the batteries in the torch or flashlight still work.

14) Preparing your cat for surgery

No matter what surgical procedure your cat is going to undergo, a good amount of preparation is mandatory. You can get all the necessary pre surgical advice from your vet. Make sure you adhere to all the guidelines.

The most common precaution to take is to ensure that your cat does not eat anything after midnight until the surgery. If you are taking a kitten for operation, on the other hand, the nutritional requirements are drastically different and you should ask your vet for guidance. Following these measures will at worst reduce the chances of complications and, at best, ensure that there are no complications during the surgery, immediately following it and later on during the recuperation phase after your Chausie has left the animal hospital.

15) *The recovery process*

Your Chausie will experience discomfort to some or other degree after the procedure. If your cat is in pain, you must make sure you either leave it under specialized care or consult your vet regularly. There are a few precautions that you can take to ensure that the recovery process is comfortable and safe.

- Give your cat a safe, quiet place in the house to rest during the recovery process. This place should not be accessible by other pets or even children.
- Do not encourage jumping, running or playing during the recovery process. You can take your Chausie out on sedate, short walks but make sure that it doesn't get physically overexerted or too tired.
- The area that has been operated on should not be licked. So, getting your cat an Elizabethan collar is the best option although the vet will probably put one on anyway.
- During the recovery process, avoid using litter or sand / soil in the litter box and rather use shredded paper. The problem with sand or litter is that the dust generated when your cat digs in it can get into a wound and cause infections or irritation.
- The site of the incision must be cleaned regularly to avoid infections.
- Look out symptoms at the site of the incision: redness, swelling in the site of the incision or discharge from the area
- Reduced appetite
- Vomiting
- Lethargy

If you do notice one or more of these symptoms, you need to inform your vet immediately.

Chapter 10: Behavioural issues

Your cat's health must be your priority. You can ensure that your Chausie stays healthy by taking it for regular vet visits, providing it with nutritious food and also ensuring that it gets enough exercise. Most physical health issues can be treated quite easily. However, if you see sudden behaviour changes in your cat, it could be suffering from some psychological disorder.

1) Sleeping habits

One of the things cats do best is sleep. On average, a healthy adult cat spends 16 or even more out of every 24 hours sleep. In other words, they spend two thirds of their time sleeping. Scientists and researchers are not quite sure why cats sleep so much.

Cats will have shorter naps and long sleeps throughout the day. No two cats will have the same sleep routines any more than people do. Sleep patterns are also affected by the weather, the cat's age, how relaxed its feeling, its general state of health, whether it's hungry or not and what its human companion is doing.

There is a fair amount of anecdotal evidence that suggests that cats are more likely to sleep when their people are not there or unavailable. Domestic cats often seem to adjust their sleep patterns in accordance with the daily rhythms of its owner and the household it lives in.

All cats will choose favourite sleeping spots. Often these will be in cool or shaded patches on a very hot day, somewhere warm and free of drafts on a cold day, and of course on a surface that is as comfortable and snuggly as possible. Cat owners have stopped being surprised to find their cat sleeping on a chair, a bed, in a draw on top of clothes, or somewhere else that is not necessarily terribly convenient for the owner.

Just like human beings, when cats sleep there is more than one type of sleep: there are periods of lighter sleep and others of much deeper sleep. Interestingly, EEG results indicate that in deep sleep there is almost as much brain activity in a cat as when it is awake.

As with many other mammals, there are also periods of REM or rapid eye movement sleep. This is also a state of deep sleep and usually the phase of sleep in which dreams occur. Do cats dream? That's impossible to determine. It seems possible, however.

2) Behaviour problems

There are a number of fairly common behavioural problems one encounters in cats including the Chausie on occasion. It is certainly best to try and nip any undesirable behaviour in the bud when you first start to notice them before they become entrenched and much harder to deal with.

Missing the litter box

One of these areas of difficulty is when your kitten or adult cat starts to miss the litter box. Before looking for a more complex reason begin with the more obvious ones. For instance, is the litter box dirty? Cats are very clean by nature and will not use a litter box that is dirty or too damp. Have you started using a different or new type of cat litter? It might be that your kitten or cat does not like the smell or feel of it. Cats also like their privacy. Is the litter box in a place where there is a lot of activity that is off-putting for your cat?

Most of the time, this particular behavioural issue can be explained by looking at the issues discussed above. Once the underlying cause has been addressed the problem behaviour usually stops.

Scratching

A second fairly common problem is a cat that scratches your furniture, carpets, curtains and even wallpaper. If you don't already have a scratching post buying one must be the first thing you do. If you do have a scratching post that your cat is not using, you will have to retrain it to do so (please see chapter 6).

Excessive scratching can also cause problems for a cat as it may bleed as the skin becomes raw or if a nail tears. It has been noted that cats use scratching as a tool to demand your attention. It is best to take note of this behaviour before your Chausie inflicts physical pain on itself.

Urinating or defecating in the house

An unfortunately common behavioural problem with cats is urination or defecation in the house. This is a very unpleasant for cat owners in terms of knowing how to deal with their cat, cleaning up the mess, stains and the various unpleasant smells – sometimes lingering ones – that go with it.

There could be a number of reasons why your cat is doing this. With urinating, the most frequent reasons are that your cat is marking the house as his or her territory, they have a medical problem, they can't or won't use the litter box for some reason or they are stressed or frightened. Once you have ruled out a medical reason you can deal with the underlying cause and the behaviour should stop.

Remember not to shout at your cat, smack him or her or rub a cat's nose in it; this will just create a fearful, stressed cat and it will not stop the behaviour. This is especially true of the Chausie which becomes very distressed if shouted at.

Attention seeking disorder

Cats with this problem will 'talk' nonstop at certain times of the day or night. Of course this is rather different with a breed that is either mute or has a very quiet voice. However, their constant chirps or attempts to speak can become distressing for the owner, family and the cat. One needs to try and understand what is causing a cat to behave in this manner. The cause for such behaviour can be either emotional or physical pain that the cat is experiencing.

Some cats produce terrible sounds as though they are in dire straights and calling out for help. This sound can make the cat owner cringe with sympathy for the poor creature. It can be a result of pain, suddenly feeling lost, deafness or even a call for help from an old or infirm cat. Some cat owners think that it can also happen when a cat wakes from a bad dream.

The reason for this behaviour need not always be an emotional one. A certain condition called as Feline Hyperesthesia is also associated with this distressing behaviour. When a cat makes these sounds during the night and is found rolling on the floor then you must consider this condition. It is more commonly known as Rippling Skin Disorder and is a stress related condition. However, the symptoms usually include a set of unrelated issues as cats with this condition tend to become extremely sensitive to touch and the skin begins to show ripples.

The possible causes of this disorder are the excessive presence of unsaturated fatty acids in combination with Vitamin E deficiency, brain infection or trauma or even flea allergies. If the cat is diagnosed with this disorder then it is unlikely that it will be completely cured. So, paying attention to these issues can help you to provide greater comfort to the cat and monitor its behavioural issues effectively and appropriately.

Chronic pseudo hunger can also cause these behaviours. They are not uncommon in cats. Like people, cats also have food cravings which are unwarranted. Cats tend to develop a strong liking for some treats such as tuna. This can also turn into an addiction. This causes the cat to beg for food all day because of cravings that are misread as hunger.

Cats that run in circles around their owner's feet are at risk of accidentally being trodden on and / or making their owner fall. This is also categorized under attention seeking issues in cats. They are much like children who need a little bit of extra attention. These cats also tend to rub themselves against your arm when they need want attention from you.

Aggression towards other cats

Many people don't get too concerned when their cats have scraps or the odd fight. An all out fight with an outsider tends to be more dramatic and taken more seriously. However, it is wise to be watchful when your cats get into a fight because you have to make sure that the fight doesn't become too serious.

Cats fight for several reasons including fear, territorial disputes or misunderstandings, competition for a female, the venting of stress, anxiety, display etc. There are various kinds of aggression that are seen in cats.

Sexual aggression in cats is a common phenomenon but it is not often seen. However, when two cats get sexually aggressive towards each other, the dominant cat bites the nape of the less dominant or the subservient cat's neck and then attempts to climb onto the subservient cat's back.

Territorial aggression is also observed quiet often amongst all animals including domestic cats. Cats mark their territory by urinating, spraying or rubbing their faces against objects. This leaves their scent or pheromones which tells other cats whose turf or territory it is.

Cats will hiss and growl to warn an intruder that he or she is unwelcome. If the intruder pays no attention to the warnings then a fight will usually take place. Fortunately, this does not occur between Chausie cats too often as they are, as a rule, less territorial than most other breeds.

Aggression directed at human beings

It is unlikely that your cat will become friendly with everybody who visits your home. Most domesticated cats are civil to guests or will simply quietly leave if they are uncomfortable in their company. However, when a cat tends to get aggressive towards people in general then it is a clear indication of the fact that the particular cat has been poorly trained when it was younger.

Biting, scratching and unpleasant vocalization are all indications of a badly trained cat or one that has not been socialised. Some possible causes of aggressive cat behaviour towards human beings are:

Overstimulation: This problem surfaces when the owner of the cat or a person does not understand the body language of the cat. There are cats that enjoy petting while others prefer to be left alone. Even the most petting-friendly cats don't like to be cuddled or stroked for unreasonable lengths of time or too hard. When they get over stimulated, they tend to scratch or bite to show that the petting session is over.

If one watches a cat closely you will see that the cat starts moving away. It might begin by pulling its ears back and narrowing its eyes. If the owner fails to understand these signals then the cat begins to lash its tail. Finally, if the owner continues the cat may become aggressive and scratch or bite.

Redirected aggression: This comes about when the cat's aggression towards his or her owner or other human beings is not necessarily due to something that person has done but to something else that has frightened or disturbed the cat. For example, when your Chausie spots a foreign cat or any other strange animal around the house there is a possibility of the cat becoming agitated and aggressive. As a reaction to this your cat will scratch or bite the first thing it can reach.

3) Going away and travelling with your Chausie

Whether you are going on a vacation or even going will in on a business trip, the biggest issue that you will face is making the right arrangements for your Chausie while you are away. You must ensure that your cat is in safe hands and is somewhere where it will be treated well and given a lot of love and affection.

There are several options that are available, but the most common and the most reliable ones are:

- *Friends*: If you are a cat lover, you will in all likelihood be in the company of several others who love, even adore, cats. There will probably be someone in your group who can pitch in to take care of your cat while you are away. When you are handing this responsibility over to a friend, make sure that he or she has had pets in the past, preferably a cat. You must look for someone who will be able to make your cat comfortable and less anxious.

- *Family*: If you have relatives who visit you regularly, leaving your cat in their care is a great idea because your cat will be familiar with the smell, sound and sight of them and will be able to adjust better in their company. If someone from your family is willing to stay over at your home and take care of your cat while you are away, it is the best possible scenario.

- *A neighbour*: If you have friendly neighbours who love cats, ask them to take care of your Chausie. Neighbours, again, will be familiar to your cat and will therefore be able to comfort it while you are away. In addition, the locality and the surroundings will not be too different for your cat to make adjustments to.

- *A pet sitter*: There are several companies and a number of individuals who will be willing to provide you with pet sitting services while you are away. You can ask for recommendations from people who have used these services in the past to choose the right company for your Chausie.

  You should meet the people who work at the company or the pet sitter before you appoint them. If you are sure that they are gentle, kind and, most importantly, responsible, you can do a trial run for one evening. If your see that they are good with your cat and that your cat is comfortable in their presence, you can give them the responsibility of taking care of your Chausie while you are away.

- *A boarding home or cattery*: There are several places where your cat will be boarded for the period that you are away. These professionals have all the necessary assistance. From people who feed and clean the cages to certified vets, you will find that all the services are provided in these shelters. Here again, you can ask for recommendations before you actually decide to place your cat in a particular shelter.

  Visit the facility to check their standards of hygiene. The conditions of the cages, the staff and the facilities available all play an important role in the decision that you make.

If you have to travel and leave your Chausie home alone, make sure that you take all the necessary steps to schedule your trip according to your cat. Plan well in advance and keep a list of options that are available to take care of your cat. Never rush these things in the last minute, as you will end up making compromises on the necessary arrangements.

One can never say when an emergency will occur. In case you have to leave suddenly, you must be able to find the best assistance for your cat's care. So, it is a good idea to make a list of people or companies who will always be willing to take care of your cat while you are away. It is a good idea to make a list of possible contacts and keep them near your phone so you can just reach out, pick the phone and make sure your cat has a safe home to stay in.

Ordinarily cats are not the best travel companions. However, your Chausie is an exception and will probably be easy to travel with. However, whether you are travelling by car or train, make sure air conditioning is available to keep your cat comfortable.

Travelling by car

If you are travelling by car remember that you must never leave your cat to wander around in the car. If your cat jumps on the driver or gets under his or her feet or the pedals, the consequences could be fatal!

Make sure that you always carry your cat in a carrier. The carrier should be extremely sturdy and must be made from metallic wires or even fibre glass. The carriers made from light plastic or even cardboard are not meant for long journeys. They are only suitable for short trips like a visit to the vet.

The weather that you travel in is extremely important in deciding what measures you need to take while travelling. If you think that it will get hotter as you proceed, make sure that you get a carrier that allows a good amount of air circulation. In case it is going to get cold along the way, carry enough blankets to wrap your Chausie up and keep it warm. There are also draft free carriers that will ensure that you do not leave your kitty shivering and uncomfortable.

Irrespective of the kind of carrier that you buy, there is one more thing that you need to consider. In case you are planning to change your mode of transport along the way, plane for example, you must also check the guidelines that they provide with respect to the type of carrier that is allowed.

If you have ample space in the back of your car and you only intend to travel by car, you can even use a large crate to keep your cat in. All you need to do is place blankets and sheets inside this crate and put it in the back of your car. The only thing that you need to ensure is that you provide your cat with a quiet place where he can rest during the journey. Place his favourite toys and treats around him to reduce the stress of travelling. The bedding that you provide during the travelling period should be what he or she is already used to.

Make sure that the crate or the carrier is completely secure. Even if you were to apply brakes suddenly it must be safe. If the carrier or crate falls suddenly or slides forward, your Chausie will be startled and might even be hurt. The last thing you want while travelling is an anxious or injured cat.

Finally, never allow the cat to be placed in the boot as this area is very dark and badly ventilated. Check on your cat regularly throughout the journey and make sure that it is comfortable.

Travelling by train

When you are travelling by train you must obviously place your cat in a carrier. Since there are several strangers on a train, you do not want to have any instances of your cat breaking free and running scared or scaring the passengers. So, make sure that the carrier that you have is extremely sturdy.

The base of the carrier must be strong to ensure that your cat is secured. The carrier itself should be light so that you do not have any difficulty carrying it around. It must also be of a convenient size depending upon the space available on the train. However, make sure that you get a carrier that is large enough for your cat to rest in. Never cram your Chausie into a small carrier because there isn't enough storage space.

You must keep a familiar blanket in the carrier to reduce anxiety. However, littering and soiling can be quite a concern. So, line your cat's cage with a good amount of absorbent paper so that you both have a pleasant journey.

Travelling by Air

Travelling with your pet by air requires a good deal of planning in advance. Not all airlines are prepared to transport cats. If they do, they are usually handled as freight. However, if you do find airlines that have the facility to transport your Chausie, you must take several precautions. For instance, don't ever transport a pregnant cat or a kitten that is younger than three months of age by air.

Check on the necessity for a license to transport animals in the airlines that you choose. Furthermore, there are chances that you and your cat will travel on separate flights. If this will be the case, you should make sure that you get a direct flight for your cat so that he or she does not have to deal with additional stressors and an even longer journey because of issues such as transits and transfers.

Find out whether you what type of proof of vaccinations and health status you need to provide. Some airline companies also insist that a cat that is going into the cargo hold must be sedated for the duration of the flight.

Travelling with your Chausie can be fun if you prepare it in advance. The most important thing to do is to condition him or her to enjoy sitting inside a carrier.

4) Why and how your cat purrs

It used to be believed that cats purr when they are content and happy. This is only part of what is apparently a far more complex and fascinating mechanism. Research now indicates that it is a means of communicating and may also be a form of self-healing.

Oddly enough a cat will also purr if it feels sick, threatened or frightened. A vet by the name of Kelly Morgan has an interesting theory: a purr is the feline equivalent of a smile in people. This makes sense as people smile when happy, sometimes to hide embarrassment, to appease the other person or even to mask anger or sadness.

How a cat purrs is also interesting. A part of the brain, a neural oscillator, sends a message to the muscles of the larynx. These muscles begin to twitch incredibly fast: 25 – 150 vibrations per second. Because of the vibrations, the vocal cords separate as the cat breathes in and out. The resulting sound is a purr.

In addition to using the purr to communicate with people and perhaps each other, bioacoustics researchers now think that purring helps cats to heal. Vibrations in the range that the vocal cords vibrate have been shown to relieve pain, heal wounds faster and even promote bone growth and increase bone density. The purring of your Chausie could well have health and healing benefits for you too.

5) *Feline stress and dealing with it*

Animals also get stressed, as people do, but they don't have the same range of options to relieve their stress that we do. Your Chausie will lower your stress levels. You need to do the same for him or her even though this breed is less prone to stress than most.

Stress has its advantages because, thanks to the adrenaline it releases, it can boost performance or even help an animal, and people, avoid injury or death. It is responsible for the important "Fight or flight" response. The danger arises when the stress is either acute or chronic; if we or a cat goes on feeling stressed for a long time there are numerous harmful effects.

The most significant of the physical consequences is damage to the immune system. A chronically stressed cat can loose its appetite, become agitated, urinate or defecate in the house, spray, begin to tremble or shiver, try to vocalise much more than usual, become very restless or even hide. Keep in mind that these symptoms could also be caused be a medical condition so you need to rule that possibility out first by having a vet check your cat.

Once you know that your Chausie isn't sick, you need to identify the stressor or cause of the stress. Have you moved recently? Has a new pet or person been introduced into your home? Is there new furniture or have you redecorated? Are you packing to go away? Has your neighbour acquired a new pet that your cat could have had contact with? Any of these changes, or a host of others, could stress some cats. Others will take it in their stride or find it fun!

Your first line of attack is to change the situation that is causing the problem. If that is not going to be possible you may need to consider removing the cat. For instance, if there are workmen in your home consider placing your Chausie with a trusted friend or at a cattery until your home is back to normal.

The next option is to help your cat change its response to stress. Spend extra time with your Chausie stroking and soothing it. Massaging cats can have a wonderfully relaxing effect on them (and you). Stroke and speak to your cat as you slowly approach the source of stress.

Don't push too hard or rush your cat; you need to acclimatize him or her gently. If necessary you can get a sedative of some sort from the vet to take the edge of the anxiety. In extreme cases some owners opt to consult a cat therapist.

6) Moving house with your cat

Moving house with a Chausie is easier than with many other breeds because they are less territorial than most and, so long as you are around, your cat should cope fairly well. However, there are still things that you need to do – or not do – to make a move as non-stressful as possible.

If you are just moving a short distance, say within the same city or town, you need to move your belongings and set up your new home first before you move your cat. That way, you can arrive with your cat in its carrier and introduce it to the new house with the familiar furniture already in place.

However, if you are moving a greater distance you will need to transport your cat in your car or on a train or plane as discussed and described in detail earlier in this chapter. Remember to always use your cat's own blanket and a toy or two for the comfort of familiar scents and objects.

If you are still arranging furniture or the movers are still moving in and out of the premises when you arrive, you must try to spare your Chausie all, or most of, the commotion and upheaval. Find a quiet, safe room in the new house where you can put him or her. Leave the carrier, a blanket, food, water and a litter box in the room. Keep the door closed or locked so he or she won't be bothered or accidently let out of the room. Remember to visit your cat regularly and make some time to pet and talk to it.

When you move into a new home you need to keep your Chausie inside even if ordinarily he or she was allowed outside at your previous home. This is a new and therefore unknown and scary environment for your cat. A real danger can be if a cat gets a fright or becomes alarmed and it is not yet familiar with its surroundings. It could run and either get lost or encounter trouble in the form of other animals or traffic in nearby roads. Your cat must, even if only initially, be a purely inside cat until you are sure that he or she is completely settled.

Of course there will be some variation from cat to cat. Some cats will settle fast and will be able – and want – to explore the whole house from the start. Others will need a room or a hiding place in which to settle and they will venture out for short exploratory trips until they are confident enough to look the whole place over.

Then there are other cats, including Chausie cats, who will settle pretty quickly so long as their owner is there. Of course there are also cats that will only emerge from hiding after being bribed, cajoled and begged.

Some cat owners find it helpful to go on a tour of the new house with their cat. If your cat is too nervous to follow you or walk with you, you could pick him or her up and do the tour together. Again, make sure to speak soothingly to your Chausie and pet him or her so it knows all is well.

As a rule, if your furniture is in place and most smells are familiar your cat will settle in well and make the necessary adjustments. If, however, your cat is of a generally more nervous disposition it might not be a bad idea to speak to your vet about a mild sedative to help your Chausie make the move more easily and with less stress.

Chapter 11: Becoming an Chausie breeder

If you want to breed Chausie cats you will need several things in addition to a passion for it: a vet who you have a good relationship with and who understands and knows the breed, lots of available time, energy, a mentor or advisor such as an established breeder, the ability to deal with some heartache and the necessary money. If you only want to breed the Chausie because you have heard there are waiting lists for them and money to be made, you are in the wrong business!

As a breeder you will need to be even more hygiene and health conscious than you are as a cat owner. The kittens especially are vulnerable when they are very young and can be prone to respiratory illnesses. In fact, one of your responsibilities will be to learn about cat illnesses. You need to read a lot, talk to vets and or breeders and get as much information as you can so that you can pick up signs or symptoms early. In other words, a breeder must know about illnesses, transmission, prevention and treatment.

It is also advisable to become a registered breeder. Find out from an internet search, your mentor, an existing breeder or your vet which associations you need to investigate and join. Membership gives you access to really useful information and a support network. It also gives you credibility as a breeder in the eyes of people who will buy kittens or cats from you.

There are also numerous very helpful – and often fun – blogs, newsletters, clubs, forums and chat rooms out there that focus on the Chausie breed. Have a look at them, join clubs and chat rooms, follow blogs or subscribe to newsletters and decide which you find useful or just enjoyable. It can be very productive to spend time in chat rooms or open blogs where Chausie breeders and owners share experiences and offer comments or advice.

There is a convention when it comes to naming a Chausie. One should use the French naming system which dictates that the first letter of the cat's name is determined by what year it was born in. The letters K, Q, W, X, Y and Z are not included and this system follows a 20 year cycle.

1) Sexual maturity

If you buy a registered Chausie kitten with a view to becoming a breeder you need to know when it is sexually mature and at what age you can start to breed with it.

Both males (toms) and females (queens) reach puberty later than most other breeds. However, as with humans there are always some variations. Some cats are only ready at about two years. You will have to establish the status or sexual maturity of your cat by its behaviour.

Females will come onto heat. When she does you will notice that she is far more affectionate and vocal than usual. She may also yowl to attract a mate. You need to keep your very young female inside and safe because you don't want her to get pregnant by a non Chausie or when she is still too young to safely have a litter.

Males that are sexually mature will also become far more vocal. They will try to get out and may also spray to mark territory and attract a female. Here again you need to keep your male cat inside until the urge to mate subsides.

Females should not be used for breeding until they are 18 to 24 months old. Males should not be used until they are 18 months old. You want a cat that is not only sexually mature but also fully grown, strong and more grown up.

2) Breeding: general pointers

The single most important activity is monitoring a female's heat cycle very carefully. When a cat is in heat, 1 or 2 eggs are released by the ovaries in a 24 hour period. If your cat's heat lasts

7 days that's 7 to 14 eggs. So, a female cat that mates each of those 5 days could well conceive on each day.

Given a week in a cat pregnancy is like a month for a human one, the kitten(s) conceived on day 7 will be born at the same time as the kitten(s) conceived on day 1. The day 7 kitten is effectively premature (in human terms it is a month premature) and therefore vulnerable to a number of potentially fatal health problems.

The solution is pretty simple: only allow your female to mate during the first half (2 or 3 days) of the heat cycle. That way all the kittens will be developed to almost identical stages and you will greatly reduce the chance of loosing kittens.

The interval between one heat cycle and another is usually about 10 days, so you should expect your female cat to exhibit this behaviour at least twice in a month during the breeding season.

The hormonal changes that take place in the cat's body in this period are tremendous. While oestrogen causes the onset of the heat cycle, progesterone takes over when she is pregnant. As the level of oestrogen increases, the heat cycle will intensify. Once the level of oestrogen drops, the heat cycle ends. This rise and fall of oestrogen will only end when she is mated.

The mating season usually starts in January or February and continues until October or. The temperature during this season and the ratio between light and dark hours will play a significant role in your cat's heat cycle.

3) Finding the right mate

Cats are extremely sensitive creatures. Most often, they will be able to choose their own mates when you take them to the breeder. If your cat has not been neutered or spayed, make sure you take them to a good breeder, especially with a pedigreed cat like the Chausie.

You must always take a queen to the tom for breeding, as she will not be too sensitive to these environmental changes during the mating process. The actual mating does not last for more than 4 minutes. Once this is over, the queen will break free by striking the male with her paw and turning away. The after-reaction of the female is cleaning herself after rolling and thrashing for a while. The after-reaction may last up to 9 minutes.

If you are interested in producing a litter, you may have to allow your cat to be mated multiple times. With a single mating, there is only a 50% chance of your cat getting pregnant. Studies show that female cats will allow up to 30 matings at intervals of 5 minutes.

One interesting fact about cats in general is that while each kitten has one father, the fathers of the kittens in a single litter may not have the same father. This is true because of the multiple mating processes. Of course this will not be the case if the queen is only covered by one tom.

Once the kittens arrive you also need to make sure both mother and babies are kept at the right temperature. You must keep the basket or nesting place out of drafts, as kittens are prone to respiratory problems when they are very little. They aren't able to regulate their body temperature the way the adults can. If they get too cold they can't digest their milk or get the nutrients they need.

4) *What to feed your pregnant cat*

The most important rule is to continue to feed your pregnant Chausie a healthy and balanced diet. A pregnant cat may ask for extra food but be strong and resist her pleas; extra food will result in weight gain which will be bad for her as it puts stress on the organs. This in turn is unhealthy for the unborn kittens.

Some vets recommend a diet that contains calcium, phosphorus and extra protein for pregnant cats. It's also been suggested by some that several small meals throughout the day is better for a pregnant cat that two larger meals each day. Your cat's eating patterns will probably change during the course of the pregnancy and when labour is very close she won't want to eat at all.

5) Gestation

The standard gestation period for cats is 62 to 65 days. There is some variation by a day or two on either side. For the first 3 to 4 weeks one often doesn't notice anything about the cat's condition. You will probably spot behaviour changes first.

A pregnant cat will become even more home loving and will probably start to sleep more. She often also becomes increasingly affectionate and demonstrative towards her owners and will actively look for attention to a marked degree.

By the 16th day of pregnancy the rounded abdomen should make it obvious that your cat is pregnant. If you are not experienced with cats, an ultrasound can help you decide if your cat is pregnant or not. There is an easy way to check. If the uterus feels stringy, it means that your cat might be pregnant.

By the 20th day of pregnancy, you can actually feel the kitten foetuses in the abdomen of the queen when she is relaxed. A while later you may be able to feel some movement.

In the fourth week of pregnancy the nipples or teats will start to become a darker pink and to protrude. In the fifth week you will notice that her tummy gradually gets rounder.

About two weeks, sometimes one, before the kittens are due the mother will begin to look for a suitable place in which to give birth. It's not a bad idea to provide a basket or a box with a towel or blanket in it in a place that is peaceful and warm.

The box or basket must be of sufficient size to allow the cat to stretch out full length. Of course in typical cat fashion you will know soon enough if what you have provided is not what she wants! Your cat may go off and select a draw or cupboard or somewhere else that is not ideal from your point of view but certainly is from hers.

Besides checking for pregnancy, ultrasound is also a useful tool to establish whether or not the development of the foetuses is normal. You can have an ultrasound performed by your vet from the 26th day of pregnancy onwards.

6) Special care for a pregnant cat

The pregnancy period is a very delicate one and you want to make sure that you do what is necessary. You must ensure that you take the best care of your Chausie so that she stays well, produces a healthy litter and has a safe and, hopefully, easy delivery.

There are a few things to keep in mind while caring for a pregnant cat:

✓ Morning sickness is very common in cats. Your vet will be able to provide you with assistance if this persists or is severe.

✓ Your pregnant cat may also reduce her food consumption by the third week of pregnancy.

✓ Overfeeding and weight gain during pregnancy can lead to complications during labour so resist giving her extra food or meals.

✓ The food that you give your pregnant queen must be highly nutritious.

✓ Protein and calcium are a must in the diet of a pregnant cat. However, never provide any supplements unless they have been recommended by a vet.

✓ Your cat should be kept indoors during the last 15 days of pregnancy. This helps you ensure that she does not give birth elsewhere.

✓ During your cat's pregnancy, you must make sure that you take her to visit the vet for regular check-ups.

✓ The most important time for your visits to the vet is during the last two weeks of pregnancy.

In addition to this, you should continue with the usual grooming routine and lavish her with a lot of love, affection and praise.

7) *Preparing for and assisting at the birth*

There are a few things that you should keep handy when your Chausie is in the last two weeks of her pregnancy:

- A sturdy box of some sort
- Surgical gloves
- Syringe or eyedropper to remove secretions from the nose and mouth.
- Cotton thread or Dental floss for the umbilical cord ties
- Antiseptic for the umbilical stumps
- Sharp, clean scissors
- Clean and fresh towels
- The vet's number
- Emergency contact numbers.

Now all you need to do is prepare for the actual birth. When your cat is in the last week of her pregnancy, place the kittening box in a quiet spot. This spot should be warm and completely draft free. Place your cat's favourite blanket and some toys in this box to encourage her to sleep there before the kittens are born.

The bedding that you choose should be comfortable for the kittens and shouldn't snag their claws. The bedding must be changed and washed regularly after the birth.

Danger signs

If you observe one or more of the following symptoms during your cat's pregnancy or the delivery you must contact your vet right away:

- A marked and sudden lack of appetite in your queen for 24 hours or more
- Your cat's temperature is high and continues to stay elevated
- She becomes lethargic and is no longer interested in anything

- There is an unpleasant smelling discharge or bleeding from the vagina.

These are all signs that something might have gone wrong during the gestation or delivery. If it is after the birth they probably indicate post-natal stress in your cat and they must be treated at the earliest opportunity.

Things not to do during pregnancy

- Never use any flea powder or medicine without consulting your vet first.
- Don't give your Chausie medication without a valid prescription.
- Do not use antiseptics suitable for humans. These products may burn your cat's delicate skin.
- Avoid handling the kittens too much. There is a chance that a mother cat will disown or even kill the kittens if they are threatened by intruders. Allow the kittens and the mother to bond.
- Allow your cat to roam around. Cats can get pregnant again within 2 weeks of delivery. It is therefore best to keep her in confinement for a while.
- Have your cat sterilised in the 7 weeks after the kittens' birth.

Taking care of a pregnant cat is a huge responsibility. If you are not sure how to go about it, you can look for a shelter or a veterinary hospital where the cat will be taken care of until the kittens are born.

Once the kittens have been born, you can decide if you want to keep them in your home or find them another loving home to live in.

8) The birth itself

You will notice that your pregnant cat starts to become rather restless at about 12 or 24 hours before she's going to give birth.

She will go back and inspect the nesting place several times, sometimes adjusting the bedding. At this point she will probably also stop eating.

The first sign that the birth is imminent is that there will be a slight discharge of clear amniotic fluid. This is the feline equivalent of water breaking. As with human beings and other animals, contractions will become stronger and closer together over time.

There is no hard and fast rule about how your cat will behave while she is in labour. Cats with very strong bonds to their humans, like the Chausie, will probably not want to be left on their own. However, more experienced mothers are quite happy to get on with it on their own in peace and quiet.

Once the cervix has opened, expulsion contractions begin. The cat will usually lie on her side or even squat, using her stomach muscles to assist the contractions. After this point the birth of the kittens occurs rapidly. Most kittens are born headfirst but almost a third of kittens are breech births with the hindquarters appearing first.

When the kitten has been born the mother will tear the amniotic sac open if it hasn't already broken. She will drink the fluid and eat the sac and then begin to lick and clean the kitten. This licking not only cleans and dries the kitten but it also stimulates the new-born's circulation and respiration.

Once all the kittens have been born the placenta is discharged or removed and eaten by the mother. If the umbilical cord has not already detached from each kitten, the mother will nibble gently through it.

The reason the mother disposes of the amniotic sac, fluid and placenta is to keep her nest clean, prevent smells and it also provides her with high quality, energy boosting food.

9) Dealing with the umbilical cord if the mother doesn't

In the unlikely event that the mother does not sever the umbilical cord herself you must do so. It's very important to remember that you need to wait 5 to 10 minutes before severing the cord. If you don't there is a risk that the kitten will suffer brain damage. This is as a result of depriving the kitten of maximum blood supply during the crucial first few minutes after birth.

Before cutting the cord, apply a ligature by tying a piece of thread or dental floss that has been soaked in disinfectant solution around the umbilical cord about 2 cm (3/4") from the kitten's body. Cut the cord with disinfected scissors 1 cm (1/3") from the ligature on the side of the placenta, not the kitten. Then you need to clean the cut end of the cord with tincture of iodine or some other disinfectant solution.

10) Feeding kittens if the mother can't or shouldn't

Sometimes a kitten has to be hand fed because the mother has died, has no milk or rejects the kitten or the kitten is too weak to suckle.

You can either purchase a kitten formula from your vet or you can make up your own. The first do-it-yourself formula contains 1 cup evaporated or powdered milk mixed with boiled water and made up to double the strength recommended for human babies. Add to the mix one egg yolk and 1 teaspoon of glucose additive. The second option is to use half a cup of cow's milk mixed with an egg yolk and 1 teaspoon of glucose. If the kitten gets diarrhoea, you need to dilute the mixture further.

Before you begin to feed the kitten make sure that the substitute milk is body temperature. During the first week of life a kitten requires about 5 ml or 1 teaspoon of milk substitute every two hours. Thereafter the frequency of feedings should be decreased and the amount of milk substitute increased. Four hourly feeding is sufficient once the kitten has reached the age of 2 weeks.

There are two methods that can be used to feed a kitten. Firstly one can do bottle feeding. With this method you should hold the kitten firmly but gently with its head elevated slightly. Move the teat of the bottle in and out of the kitten's mouth and express a small amount of milk to encourage the kitten to develop a sucking response.

If you are dealing with a very small and weak kitten you may need to resort to stomach tube feeding. It is strongly recommended that you consult your local vet for a demonstration of the correct way to do this so that no damage is accidentally done to the oesophagus or any other internal organs or tissue.

Chapter 12: The aging Chausie cat

1) The ageing Chausie

As with any other species, humans included, aging brings an increasing number of health problems and general deterioration. The ageing process can't be stopped, but there are some things we can do to minimise the effects and to make a cat's life as happy and comfortable as possible.

Age related changes

The changes you will see in your cat include:

- *Claws*: while some body processes are slowing down, cat's claws actually grow faster as they get older so it is necessary to trim their nails more frequently.

- *Feeding and drinking*: an older cat may experience a loss of appetite or be reluctant to eat. Problems with their teeth or gums could also cause difficulty. Older cats also feel thirsty more often than younger cats.

- *Digestive problems*: your cat may not be able to process food the way it did or tolerate the same kinds of food it did when it was younger. To deal with these issues it can be helpful to feed your cat three or four small meals a day, increase the amount of moist foods in the diet or move to special or prescription food. Your vet will be able to advise you about the best one for your Chausie.

- *Sleep*: ageing cats will want and need to sleep even more than their younger counterparts. In addition, their sleep is often deeper and your cat is likely to be very startled if woken suddenly. Wherever possible, allow your elderly feline friend to sleep quietly and undisturbed.

- *Weight loss*: this often occurs gradually – over a period of several months – and you might not even notice this change in your cat at first. The weight loss occurs even when the cat continues to eat well.

- *Joint changes*: arthritis and osteoarthritis will cause your cat to move stiffly when he or she first gets or wakes up. In more the advanced stages of these conditions, a cat may have difficulty walking and jumping up onto surfaces such as beds and chairs. As soon as you notice these symptoms in your Chausie, take him or her to the vet for treatment or at least symptomatic and pain relief.

- *Constipation*: if your cat is an outdoors cat, you may not notice that he or she is having this difficulty. It is important, however, not to allow constipation to continue as it could result in a potentially dangerous bowel blockage or obstruction. Cat laxative products are available from vets some of which can be added to the cat's food. Many vets caution against the use of medicinal paraffin for cats.

- *Blindness*: usually a cat's eye sight will deteriorate gradually. Signs to look out for are white patches near the centre of the eye or a bluish, slightly opaque film over the eye. Once the cat's eyesight has become a really bad you will notice him or her starting to walk into furniture and showing reluctance to go out. All you can do is take steps to protect your cat from obvious dangers like stairs and swimming pools and not change the environment, for instance don't move furniture around.

- *Deafness*: like failing eyesight, loss of hearing also usually happens over an extended period of time. It may take a while for you to notice that your Chausie does not respond to noises or to being called. This makes them more at risk if they are outdoors as they won't hear other animals or cars approaching.

- *Senility*: if your cat suffers from this condition you will notice that he or she will seem particularly restless and disorientated. There may also be increased meowing or crying and demand for your attention as your cat seeks comfort and reassurance.

In other words, even your Chausie will want more attention than usual. You need to be patient, loving and understanding and involve your vet as and when necessary.

2) How to make your aging Chausie comfortable

While you can do very little about some of the symptoms and problems your cat will face, there are certain things you can do to reduce your cat's discomfort and stress.

Firstly, monitor your cat's food and drink intake. If necessary, heat your cat's food slightly to encourage it to eat. Alternatively, introduce something new into the diet. If your cat is being very inactive and sleeping a great deal you need to decrease its food intake slightly. If you don't, he or she will put on weight and this can lead to other health problems. Also, if possible, be aware of bowel activity and urination.

Secondly, place your cat's bed and bedding in a quiet spot that is not in direct sun and drafts and where it is fairly close to the litter box if your Chausie is using one.

Next, you should accompany your elderly cat into outdoor areas or other places where he or she may encounter difficulties or dangers, especially if your cat has poor vision and / or hearing. This helps to protect it from possible accidents and decreases the cat's stress levels.

Finally, take your aging cat to the vet for regular check-ups and monitoring. You also need to maintain vaccinations and all the standard health and hygiene routines as an older cat will be more vulnerable to infections.

3) How do you know it's time to let go?

One response to this question that struck a cord is that it is time to say goodbye to your elderly Chausie companion when he or she no longer responds to you and seems to get no pleasure from life. Certainly nobody wants to see a creature they love suffering or fading away.

The Downing Centre for Animal Pain Management drew up a scale to measure animal's quality of life. The test itself was developed by a veterinary oncologist. The criteria the test uses are: pain levels, the ability to eat enough to prevent hunger or malnutrition, the ability to drink and stay hydrated, the ability to groom or be groomed and the cat's ability to move around or be mobile.

In other words, the scale looks at pain levels, appetite and the ability to eat, the ability to drink, whether the cat can still groom itself, if there is evidence that the cat can still enjoy activities and interactions with people and other animals, that he or she can walk or move around with relative ease and, finally, if the cat has more days that are good than ones that are bad.

Each criterion should be rated on a scale of 1 to 10 with 10 being ideal, for example pain-free would be 10. If your cat scores more than 35 then its quality of life is still acceptable. A score below that and you need to start considering euthanasia.

Chapter 13: Prices and costs

1) How to choose a breeder

Taking the time to do some research to find good and reputable Chausie breeders is well worth it. A good place to start is with TICA as they usually have breeder lists on their websites or available. In fact, the more investigating you do, and the more people you talk to, the better as one can't have too much information.

In addition to being able to find breeders details on the Internet, you will also be able to locate the "bad breeder list". Knowing which breeder not to go to is as useful as knowing which ones to approach. You could also join Chausie forums online and follow or contribute to blogs. Chatting to Chausie owners could also provide you with very valuable information.

How do you recognize a reputable breeder? There is no way of choosing a breeder that is 100% safe or fool proof, but there are some things that you can look out for.

A reputable breeder:

- Will be able to show you references
- Won't sell kittens younger than 12 weeks old
- Will show you around his or her facility
- Won't have multiple litters available at the same time
- Will be able to provide proof of vaccinations and so on
- Won't sell kittens to pet stores
- Will breed using pedigreed cats and cat prove it
- Won't sell kittens for a far lower price than the average
- Will offer a health guarantee on kittens.

Taking time to select the right breeder is a crucial first step in finding a healthy Chausie that is right for you. Don't rush.

2) *The cost to purchase a Chausie cat or kitten*

The price of Chausie kittens varies from breeder to breeder and from country to country. Even within countries there can be regional differences. In addition, pricing on Chausie cats can be affected by bloodlines. One will pay more for a cat that comes from show stock or that can be used for breeding than a cat with a less illustrious family tree. These cats are still relatively hard to come by and are a new breed. This means they are not inexpensive.

At time of writing the price range was large: from $500 or £335 to $2000 or £1340 per kitten. One can sometimes find an adult cat that requires rehoming for considerably less.

A word of caution: if you see 'purebred' kittens advertised for less than the average price each they are may well be the products of 'kitten mills' and should be avoided. The so-called breeder should be reported to your local cat or Chausie association and an animal welfare organization.

3) *Monthly costs of caring for your cat*

Monthly costs will be determined by a wide range of factors including your location, choice of brands and products, your kitten or cat's age and its state of health. If you own a Chausie you need to be able to accommodate these regular expenses:

- ✓ Good quality cat food
- ✓ Grooming products
- ✓ Vaccination and deworming costs
- ✓ Cat litter
- ✓ Toys
- ✓ Food and water bowls
- ✓ Treats
- ✓ (Sometimes high) vet bills following illness or injury
- ✓ Pet insurance (optional).

Once-off expenses will include registration (if necessary), having your Chausie spayed or neutered, micro-chipping and a cat carrier.

There are also items that will have to be replaced from time to time such as beds and bedding, scratching posts, toys and food and water bowls. The once-off costs, at time of writing, were in the region of:

- A litter box: $3-20 / £3-28
- Carrier: $20-50 / £15-45
- Toys: average $3 / £2.50 each
- Food and water bowls: $4-10 / £1-10
- Scratch post: $ / £4-110

Monthly costs were:

- Food: $17 / £15
- Cat litter: $10 / £12
- Grooming and flea control: $10 / £8
- Vet: $28 / £32 (based on vaccines and annual check-up)

  Total: $65 / £67

Owning a pet is a big financial responsibility. If you think that you might have to compromise on any of the expenses mentioned above, make sure you re-think your decision of bringing home a Chausie or indeed any cat. Having one of these cats will involve costs but everybody who owns one feels that it is money well spent.

4) The option to take out Pet Insurance

If you give your Chausie the right diet, perform all the necessary grooming and dental care and get vaccinations done as and when required, your cat should stay pretty healthy. Of course, no cat is completely safe from illness and even the healthiest cat can be injured. Cats are also living longer now and so they suffer from illnesses associated with age. In addition, vet care is becoming more expensive.

Enter pet insurance. Depending on where you are you may be able to opt to take out one of several types of cover to help you with bills when your cat needs medical care. Some insurers offer the choice of a plan that covers expenses in the event of an accident only. Others will pay costs for both accident and illness. The third option, one that usually gets added onto one of the others, is to cover routine procedures and costs such as vaccinations, deworming, dental descaling and sterilisations.

Like most insurance, these policies will have a deductible or excess that you will have to pay, but they can help greatly if your Chausie ever requires significant or ongoing treatment or vet care. The premium and affordability will also vary depending on the type of cover chosen and how many pets you place on the policy.

Your vet should be able to supply you with a brochure, pamphlet or information. You will have to weigh the cost of insurance against the possibility of being out of pocket at a later date.

Chapter 14: General advice & tips

Mistakes made by new Chausie owners

If you have just got yourself a Chausie you must make its care and safety your priority. When you bring home a new cat, you get so caught up in settling it in and then playing with and petting it that you can loose sight of some important aspects. There are in fact several mistakes that new cat owners make.

If you take cat care too lightly, there is a chance that your cat will not be happy and satisfied in your home. Here are some of the most concerning mistakes a Chausie owner could make:

Underestimating the cost of owning a cat

Of course, bringing home a cat is not as expensive as bringing home a dog. This, however, does not mean that it is easy to have a cat at home. The expenses of taking care of the cat, its health and also the facilities that it requires can be significant.

In addition to that, cats are a big responsibility. You will have to think twice before you plan a vacation or holiday. You will have to plan your entire schedule around your Chausie. If you are unable or unwilling to do that, owning a cat could be a serious problem for you.

Ignoring visits to the vet

You must make sure that you make a schedule of all the necessary visits to the veterinarian. If you neglect to do so there is a good chance that your cat may not get the necessary vaccinations on time or at all. In addition, you might not notice the symptoms and signs of potentially hazardous diseases.

Going to the vet will also help you understand if your routine with your cat is correct or not. In case you need to make changes in the diet, tooth care or other grooming or the amount of exercise that your cat gets, your vet can provide you with the assistance you require before problems occur.

Failure to spay or neuter your Chausie

Breeding or mating is not the easiest thing to do with cats. In case you have ignored spaying or neutering, you will find your home in a mess during the time that your cat is in heat. It is common for male Chausie cats to want to roam. Female cats, on the other hand, will keep the entire household on their feet with constant purring and yowling when they are in heat.

The worst thing that can happen to you is a litter of kittens when you are not prepared for. Being unable to care for a pregnant cat or the kittens can be very stressful for you and your cat.

Buying cheap cat food

If you try to save money on cat food remember that you will probably end up paying a great deal more to help your cat recover from nutrition related health issues or even IBD. Remember that the cat food you select must be a good source of proteins, vitamins and minerals. If you are unable to do that, your Chausie will be malnourished and unhealthy.

Cheaper varieties of cat food will only be able to provide your cat with plant based proteins. For an animal that is a carnivore, and with the Chausie may also have a shorter than normal intestine, the only good source of protein is animal protein. In addition to this, the cheap pet foods contain large amounts of carbohydrates that can make your cat sick, obese or diabetic. Make sure you only bring home high quality foods for your pet.

Allowing your cat to roam outside

By nature, a Chausie likes to stay indoors. If you let it loose outside there are chances that he or she will eat food or substances that are poisonous or hazardous to his or her health. Your cat may also be attacked by bigger animals and get hurt or infected.

Domesticated cats are not aggressive or defensive enough to take care of themselves in the great outdoors. It is true that your cat will get a lot of exercise outside. However, unsupervised visits outside the house are not recommended.

Neglecting litter box hygiene

Cats are very fussy about hygiene. If you do not clean the litter box regularly you will notice peculiar behaviour patterns like littering in other places inside the house. Some cats will also not eat well if the litter box hygiene is not maintained appropriately. Examine the litter box daily and ensure that the litter is replaced on a regular basis.

Thinking your Chausie is a human being

No matter how intelligent, loving, funny and so on your cat is she or he is… a cat. Conversely, your cat may well view you as a large not terribly athletic cat. This means that you have to try and view things from your cat's point of view. Your cat will have a reason for doing the things it does. It's part of the cat owner's job to work out what those reasons are.

Hitting your Chausie

Don't ever hit your cat. There is never anything positive to be gained from this. Although they are intelligent creatures, you can't be sure that your cat will know why it is being smacked. The result you are likely to have is a cat that becomes fearful of you and anxious.

If you need to discipline your cat, do so when you catch it 'in the act'. You can clap your hands, use a firm tone when saying "No" or even spray the cat lightly with water.

Conclusion

The Chausie is a unique creature. This breed is beautiful, active, playful, intelligent, affectionate and very loving. The Chausie also gets on well with other animals, both dogs and cats, and with children. It is also very 'bouncy' and demanding with an inability to tolerate being on its own for long. But, it is easy to handle if you set boundaries at the outset and are consistent. It will be a loving, loyal and robust companion to you for many years.

They are also very easy to groom. If you can't give your cat time and love and groom him or her, don't get a Chausie. In fact, you should probably reconsider getting a cat at all. If you want a cat that is docile or very independent then the Chausie is not for you.

If you already have a Chausie in your life I hope you have gained some useful new information and insights. If you were undecided about the breed I trust you are closer to a decision. If you are going to buy a Chausie, I hope the information here helps to prepare you!

Here is a final checklist to make sure you do not miss anything and do your best for your cat:

- Keep an eye on your pet. Be sensitive to the changes that your cat undergoes physically and mentally.

- Adapt your home so that your Chausie is never in danger from toxic substances, open heat sources and other everyday dangers.

- Make time to play and cuddle: If your work comes first, do not even try to tell your Chausie that. They do not understand how you could possibly be too busy to play with them for a brief period each day.

- Feed him or her well: You must keep a schedule and make sure that someone is always around to feed your cat on time.

Unlike humans who would eat just about anything at any time of the day, cats are highly disciplined creatures.

- Make sure that your cat always has fresh water. It is essential that cats drink enough and are encouraged to do so.

- Keep the litter box very clean for the sake of your cat, yourself and your family.

- Get all the necessary identification to ensure that your Chausie does not end up in a shelter. Consider having your cat micro-chipped but, at the very least, get a tear-away collar with an identification disc.

- Your cat's health is a priority. No matter how tired or lazy you feel, you need to make sure you take your pet to the vet at the scheduled times for vaccinations, deworming, etc. Any negligence in this area can have serious and really costly repercussions for your Chausie and for you.

I hope you savour every minute of being the proud owner of a Chausie. With this gorgeous breed in your home, you will be the envy of your entire social circle. But above all, you have a companion who will love you as long as he or she lives.

Published by IMB Publishing 2015